D0616919

ISBN 978-0-578-41159-0
90000>
9 780578 411590

The Four-Minute Prayer Journal

Helping you count your blessings, live a life of gratitude and praise, and develop a more intimate relationship with God.

The Four-Minute Prayer Journal

GET IN TOUCH:

hello@liveinprayer.com

FOR SALES INQUIRIES:

sales@liveinprayer.com

Created by Justin Froeber

ISBN: 978-0-578-41159-0
Published by Live in Prayer, LLC.

Printed in China

Live In Prayer
www.LiveInPrayer.com

DEDICATION

To all the prayer warriors in the world:
Thank you for changing the world one prayer at a time.

CONTENTS

"Rather than set aside daily time for prayer, I pray constantly and spontaneously about everything I encounter on a daily basis. When someone shares something with me, I'll often simply say, 'let's pray about this right now.'"

-Thomas Kinkade

"God is looking for people to use, and if you can get usable, he will wear you out. The most dangerous prayer you can pray is this: 'Use me.'"

- Rick Warren

"Prayer is not asking. Prayer is putting oneself in the hands of God, at His disposition, and listening to His voice in the depth of our hearts."

-Mother Teresa

"Prayer makes a godly man, and puts within him the mind of Christ, the mind of humility, of self-surrender, of service, of pity, and of prayer. If we really pray, we will become more like God, or else we will quit praying."

-E.M. Bound

“Prayer is simply talking to God like a friend and should be the easiest thing we do each day.”

-Joyce Meyer

The Four-Minute Prayer Journal

Helping you count your blessings, live a life of gratitude and praise, and develop a more intimate relationship with God.

Welcome to Your Prayer Journal!

It's a simple, easy way to encourage the habit of prayer, while positively impacting your day, and spreading the love of Christ:
By starting and ending each day with a heart of gratitude towards God's blessings and incredible mercies on your life, you set yourself up to approach life with a positive and contagiously grateful attitude; helping you become a shining, joyful light unto others.

Look Back on Your Prayers and Count Your Blessings:
You will have a time lapse of your days, weeks, months, and years. A twice-daily snapshot of the work God is doing in your life. The Four-Minute Prayer Journal gives you a written record so you can flip back to any moment in time and reflect on all the prayers you have prayed and count the blessings you have received.

It's a tool to help you lay down your burdens, anxieties, and fears and focus on the positive: We are called to lay our struggles at the feet of Jesus and take comfort in knowing that He has our best interest in mind. Using principles of positive psychology the journal is designed to help you place your burdens on the cross, while affirming your strength in Christ, and guiding you to live life with a heart of gratitude.

You don't have to be a seasoned journaler or master of prayerful prose: Prayer is simple, but we often overcomplicate it. This journal takes us back to the simple biblical guidance Jesus provided on prayer. Designed to help you eliminate excuses for not keeping a journal or being consistent in your prayer life, the Four-Minute Prayer Journal helps you develop the habit of having regular conversations with your best pal: Jesus.

The Morning Prayer Routine

Morning Prayer Routine

"In the morning, Lord, you hear my voice; in the morning I lay my requests before you and wait expectantly."

-Psalm 5:3

Morning Prayer requests

There is no better way to start the day than spending time with your Lord and Savior. Morning prayer grounds us so that we can approach the day with a Christ like heart and can hear from the Lord so that he may guide our footsteps throughout the day. And guess what?.......Jesus did it too:

Before daybreak the next morning, Jesus got up and went out to an isolated place to pray.

-Mark 1:35

As you begin your morning prayers here are a few tips to help you get started:

Find a quiet place: Grab your morning cup of brew, your bible, and your prayer journal and head to a quiet place. Find a place where you can be free from distraction and without interruption. Turn off your cell phone.

Intercede on behalf of others: Jesus did all things to the benefit of others and as followers, we should mirror his actions by selflessly praying for others. Genuine, prayerful intercession is a life giving and powerful form of prayer not only for you, but for everyone around you. If we only use prayer as a means of personal fulfillment and happiness we will never understand nor experience the true power of prayer.

Ask for Guidance: Sometimes we need a little encouragement and wisdom to have the confidence just to put one foot in front of the other. Ask for the wisdom, strength, and heart to approach the day.

I rise early, before the sun is up;
I cry out for help and put my hope in your words.

-Psalm 119:147

Expression of Gratitude

What can you be thankful and grateful for today?

God fills our lives with blessings and no matter our circumstances we can find reasons to be thankful. Each of us is truly blessed and loved by God.

Start your day by counting your blessings and expressing your thankfulness and gratitude. This will help you approach the day with a positive attitude. A grateful heart is a joyous one. And a heart of joy spreads much needed love in the world.

And by the way, what parent doesn't love a heartfelt expression of gratitude from their child? In the same manner, it warms God's heart when his children offer prayers of thanks.

….So say a big thank you to the big guy upstairs!

Affirmation of Strength

"I can do everything through him who gives me strength"
-Philippians 4:13

We have all heard you can do anything through the power of Christ, but sometimes we need to remind ourselves that he is walking with us.

Facing a big and overwhelming task at work? Struggling with family problems you do not know how to solve? Need to have a tough conversation with a friend? No matter what you are facing take comfort knowing that Jesus and the Holy Spirit are riding shotgun.

Start the day by affirming that because of your strength in Christ you are fully capable of facing whatever comes your way. Remind yourself in prayer that your Father has you in his hands. Ask for the strength and wisdom to face the trials, tribulations, and temptations. Take comfort knowing that you will receive it.

Every time you write down your daily affirmation you are not only building your faith in Christ, but building Christ driven self-confidence.

…So go ahead affirm yourself and your Lord and Savior!

"Satisfy us in the morning with your steadfast love, so that we may rejoice and be glad all our days. Make us glad as many days as you have afflicted us, and as many years as we have seen evil. Let your work be manifest to your servants, and your glorious power to their children. Let the favor of the Lord our God be upon us, and prosper for us the work of our hands - O prosper the work of our hands!"

-Psalm 90: 14-17

Finish by Listening

"To have God speak to the heart is a majestic experience, an experience that people may miss if they monopolize the conversation and never pause to hear God's responses."

-Charles Stanley

Prayer in its simplest form is a constant conversation between you and God. A conversation takes place between two people. If we never stop to let God respond are we truly opening our hearts and minds up to divine intercession?

He may not answer right away, but you should be mindful of stopping to listen. As you bring your morning prayer time to a close, build the habit of pausing just to listen.

The Evening Prayer Routine

Evening Prayer Routine

*"By day the Lord directs his love, at night his song is with me—
a prayer to the God of my life."*

-Psalm 42:8

Evening Gratitude

"Finally, brothers, whatever is true, whatever is noble, whatever is right, whatever is pure, whatever is lovely, whatever is admirable—if anything is excellent or praiseworthy—think about such things."

-Philippians 4:8

During the day you experienced God's favor far more than you could ever realize. There were some new blessings, new mercies, and maybe even some long-awaited answered prayers – an abundance of things to be thankful and grateful for!

Finish the day by thanking God for all that He is doing in your life. Count your blessings and reflect on God's goodness. Express your gratitude.

Going to bed with a grateful heart helps set the tone for a good night's rest and sets you up for a joy filled and tranquil morning.

"It is good to give thanks to the LORD, to sing praises to your name, O Most High; to declare your steadfast love in the morning, and your faithfulness by night..."

-Psalm 92:1-2

Evening Prayer Requests

"Come to me, all you who are weary and burdened,
and I will give you rest."

-Matthew 11:28`

At night, before you go to sleep, examine your conscience, inquiring into your thoughts, words, and deeds of the day. Pray prayers of thanks and gratitude and ask the Lord to guide your heart and mind.

Praying before you go to bed can help ease your mind from the troubles of the day. Laying your trials and tribulations at the feet of Christ frees you from your anxieties and worries.

Prayer can heal emotional wounds and help you control rampant thoughts that work to keep you awake and distracted. Pray that the Lord will deliver you from anxiety and depression. Ask Him to ease your mind and help you to focus on His thoughts and His ways as you lay to rest. Take comfort knowing that your prayers are heard.

"Compose yourself to rest in such a way that sleep may steal upon you with your thoughts fixed on divine things, and your mind preparing itself to spend the next day in greater holiness. Always keep in mind that saying of our heavenly Master: "What shall it profit a man if he gain the whole world, and suffer the loss of his soul?"

-Mark 8:36

Place your burdens, anxieties, concerns, and worries at the feet of Christ and rest in the goodness of the Lord!

Finish by Listening

"To have God speak to the heart is a majestic experience, an experience that people may miss if they monopolize the conversation and never pause to hear God's responses."

-Charles Stanley

Prayer in its simplest form is a constant conversation between you and God. A conversation takes place between two people. If we never stop to let God respond, are we truly opening our hearts and minds up to divine intercession?

He may not answer right away, but you should be mindful of stopping to listen. As you bring your evening prayer time to a close, build the habit of pausing just to listen.

Staying Committed to Prayer Journaling

Find a way to help keep yourself accountable for spending time in prayer and writing in your prayer journal:

1. We created a motivating and helpful series of emails to help you stick with the *Four-Minute Prayer Journal* and develop the habit of daily prayer. Go to www.prayerjournalhabits.com and sign up!

2. If you have a copy of the *Live In Prayer Planner,* use the habit tracker to check off every day that you successfully devoted time to prayer and journaling. Sometimes there is nothing more motivating than a visual reminder.

3. Find a prayer partner. Pick a close friend or significant other to check on you daily. If you receive the *Four Minute Prayer Journal* as a gift the person that gave it to you may make the perfect accountability partner.

4. Set morning and evening reminders on your smartphone to help you designate a specific time each day to prayer journaling.

5. Join the Live In Prayer Facebook group to find prayer partners and join a world-wide community of prayer warriors.

Everybody has a different style of accountability. Head over to www.prayerjournalhabits.com for more tips. Just choose the accountability method that works best for you!

Your Prayer Journal

Date ___ / ___ / ___

This is the confidence we have in approaching God:
that if we ask anything according to his will, he hears us.

-1 John 5:14

Father, I lift up the following in prayer as I start my day…

1. ______________________________
2. ______________________________
3. ______________________________

Father, I am thankful and grateful for….

1. ______________________________
2. ______________________________
3. ______________________________

Today I know you will you give me the strength to….

1. ______________________________

I praise you for all your mercies and blessings from today…

1. ______________________________
2. ______________________________
3. ______________________________

I lay the following prayers at your feet as I rest in your goodness…

1. ______________________________
2. ______________________________
3. ______________________________

Date ___ / ___ / ___

The Lord is my strength and my defense;
he has become my salvation.

-Psalm 118:4

Father, I lift up the following in prayer as I start my day…

1. ______________________________
2. ______________________________
3. ______________________________

Father, I am thankful and grateful for….

1. ______________________________
2. ______________________________
3. ______________________________

Today I know you will you give me the strength to….

1. ______________________________

I praise you for all your mercies and blessings from today…

1. ______________________________
2. ______________________________
3. ______________________________

I lay the following prayers at your feet as I rest in your goodness…

1. ______________________________
2. ______________________________
3. ______________________________

Date ___ / ___ / ___

Let the peace of Christ rule in your hearts, since as members of one body you were called to peace. And be thankful.

-Colossians 3:15

Father, I lift up the following in prayer as I start my day…

1. ______________________________
2. ______________________________
3. ______________________________

Father, I am thankful and grateful for….

1. ______________________________
2. ______________________________
3. ______________________________

Today I know you will you give me the strength to….

1. ______________________________

I praise you for all your mercies and blessings from today…

1. ______________________________
2. ______________________________
3. ______________________________

I lay the following prayers at your feet as I rest in your goodness…

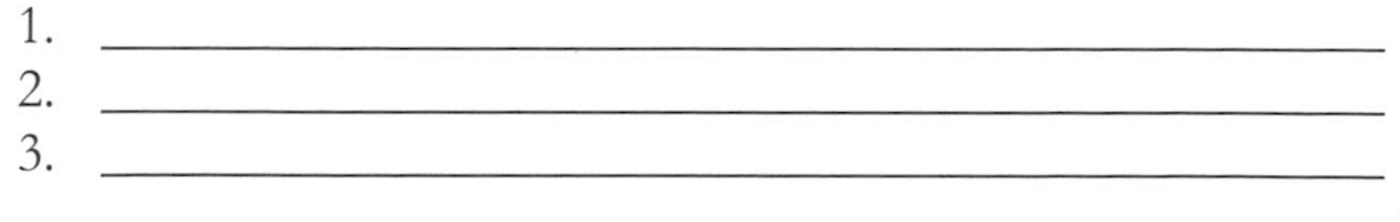

Date ___ / ___ / ___

Commit to the Lord whatever you do,
and he will establish your plans.

-Proverbs 16:3

Father, I lift up the following in prayer as I start my day…

1. ___
2. ___
3. ___

Father, I am thankful and grateful for….

1. ___
2. ___
3. ___

Today I know you will you give me the strength to….

1. ___

I praise you for all your mercies and blessings from today…

1. ___
2. ___
3. ___

I lay the following prayers at your feet as I rest in your goodness…

1. ___
2. ___
3. ___

Date ___ / ___ / ___

And my God will meet all your needs according to his glorious riches in Christ Jesus

-Philippians 4:19

Father, I lift up the following in prayer as I start my day…

1. ______________________________
2. ______________________________
3. ______________________________

Father, I am thankful and grateful for….

1. ______________________________
2. ______________________________
3. ______________________________

Today I know you will you give me the strength to….

1. ______________________________

I praise you for all your mercies and blessings from today…

1. ______________________________
2. ______________________________
3. ______________________________

I lay the following prayers at your feet as I rest in your goodness…

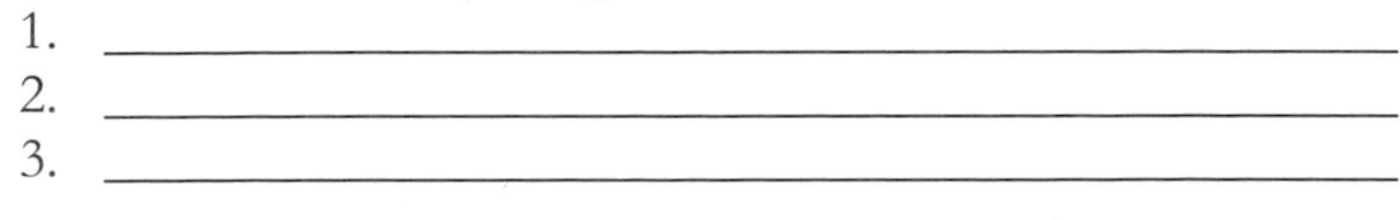

1. ______________________________
2. ______________________________
3. ______________________________

Date ___ / ___ / ___

Watch and pray so that you will not fall into temptation.
The spirit is willing, but the flesh is weak.

-Matthew 26:41

Father, I lift up the following in prayer as I start my day…

1. ______________________________
2. ______________________________
3. ______________________________

Father, I am thankful and grateful for….

1. ______________________________
2. ______________________________
3. ______________________________

Today I know you will you give me the strength to….

1. ______________________________

I praise you for all your mercies and blessings from today…

1. ______________________________
2. ______________________________
3. ______________________________

I lay the following prayers at your feet as I rest in your goodness…

1. ______________________________
2. ______________________________
3. ______________________________

Date ___ / ___ / ___

You will keep in perfect peace him whose mind is steadfast, because they trust in you

-Isaiah 26:3

Father, I lift up the following in prayer as I start my day…

1. ______________________________
2. ______________________________
3. ______________________________

Father, I am thankful and grateful for….

1. ______________________________
2. ______________________________
3. ______________________________

Today I know you will you give me the strength to….

1. ______________________________

I praise you for all your mercies and blessings from today…

1. ______________________________
2. ______________________________
3. ______________________________

I lay the following prayers at your feet as I rest in your goodness…

1. ______________________________
2. ______________________________
3. ______________________________

Date ___ / ___ / ___

And without faith it is impossible to please God, because anyone who comes to him must believe that he exists and that he rewards those who earnestly seek him.

-Hebrews 11:6

Father, I lift up the following in prayer as I start my day…

1. ______________________________
2. ______________________________
3. ______________________________

Father, I am thankful and grateful for….

1. ______________________________
2. ______________________________
3. ______________________________

Today I know you will you give me the strength to….

1. ______________________________

I praise you for all your mercies and blessings from today…

1. ______________________________
2. ______________________________
3. ______________________________

I lay the following prayers at your feet as I rest in your goodness…

1. ______________________________
2. ______________________________
3. ______________________________

Date ___ / ___ / ___

But I have trusted in Your loving devotion;
my heart will rejoice in Your salvation.

-Psalm 13:5

Father, I lift up the following in prayer as I start my day…

1. ______________________________
2. ______________________________
3. ______________________________

Father, I am thankful and grateful for….

1. ______________________________
2. ______________________________
3. ______________________________

Today I know you will you give me the strength to….

1. ______________________________

I praise you for all your mercies and blessings from today…

1. ______________________________
2. ______________________________
3. ______________________________

I lay the following prayers at your feet as I rest in your goodness…

1. ______________________________
2. ______________________________
3. ______________________________

Date ___ / ___ / ___

But God demonstrates his own love for us in this:
While we were still sinners, Christ died for us.

-Romans 5:8

Father, I lift up the following in prayer as I start my day…

1. ______________________________
2. ______________________________
3. ______________________________

Father, I am thankful and grateful for….

1. ______________________________
2. ______________________________
3. ______________________________

Today I know you will you give me the strength to….

1. ______________________________

I praise you for all your mercies and blessings from today…

1. ______________________________
2. ______________________________
3. ______________________________

I lay the following prayers at your feet as I rest in your goodness…

1. ______________________________
2. ______________________________
3. ______________________________

Date ___ / ___ / ___

Your word is a lamp for my feet,
a light on my path.

-Psalm 119:105

Father, I lift up the following in prayer as I start my day…

1. ______________________________
2. ______________________________
3. ______________________________

Father, I am thankful and grateful for….

1. ______________________________
2. ______________________________
3. ______________________________

Today I know you will you give me the strength to….

1. ______________________________

I praise you for all your mercies and blessings from today…

1. ______________________________
2. ______________________________
3. ______________________________

I lay the following prayers at your feet as I rest in your goodness…

1. ______________________________
2. ______________________________
3. ______________________________

Date ___ / ___ / ___

Be strong and courageous. Do not be afraid or terrified because of them, for the Lord your God goes with you; he will never leave you nor forsake you.

-Deuteronomy 31:6

Father, I lift up the following in prayer as I start my day…

1. ______________________________
2. ______________________________
3. ______________________________

Father, I am thankful and grateful for….

1. ______________________________
2. ______________________________
3. ______________________________

Today I know you will you give me the strength to….

1. ______________________________

I praise you for all your mercies and blessings from today…

1. ______________________________
2. ______________________________
3. ______________________________

I lay the following prayers at your feet as I rest in your goodness…

1. ______________________________
2. ______________________________
3. ______________________________

Date ___ / ___ / ___

In the same way, let your light shine before men,
that they may see your good deeds and praise your Father in heaven.

-Matthew 5:16

Father, I lift up the following in prayer as I start my day…

1. ______________________________
2. ______________________________
3. ______________________________

Father, I am thankful and grateful for….

1. ______________________________
2. ______________________________
3. ______________________________

Today I know you will you give me the strength to….

1. ______________________________

I praise you for all your mercies and blessings from today…

1. ______________________________
2. ______________________________
3. ______________________________

I lay the following prayers at your feet as I rest in your goodness…

1. ______________________________
2. ______________________________
3. ______________________________

Date ___ / ___ / ___

Keep this Book of the Law always on your lips; meditate on it day and night, so that you may be careful to do everything written in it. Then you will be prosperous and successful.

-Joshua 1:8

Father, I lift up the following in prayer as I start my day…

1. ______________________________
2. ______________________________
3. ______________________________

Father, I am thankful and grateful for….

1. ______________________________
2. ______________________________
3. ______________________________

Today I know you will you give me the strength to….

1. ______________________________

I praise you for all your mercies and blessings from today…

1. ______________________________
2. ______________________________
3. ______________________________

I lay the following prayers at your feet as I rest in your goodness…

1. ______________________________
2. ______________________________
3. ______________________________

Date ___ / ___ / ___

The Lord will rescue his servants; no one who takes refuge in him will be condemned.

-Psalm 106:2

Father, I lift up the following in prayer as I start my day…

1. ______________________________
2. ______________________________
3. ______________________________

Father, I am thankful and grateful for….

1. ______________________________
2. ______________________________
3. ______________________________

Today I know you will you give me the strength to….

1. ______________________________

I praise you for all your mercies and blessings from today…

1. ______________________________
2. ______________________________
3. ______________________________

I lay the following prayers at your feet as I rest in your goodness…

1. ______________________________
2. ______________________________
3. ______________________________

Date ___ / ___ / ___

Wait for the Lord; be strong and take heart
and wait for the Lord.

-Psalm 27:14

Father, I lift up the following in prayer as I start my day…

1. ______________________________
2. ______________________________
3. ______________________________

Father, I am thankful and grateful for….

1. ______________________________
2. ______________________________
3. ______________________________

Today I know you will you give me the strength to….

1. ______________________________

I praise you for all your mercies and blessings from today…

1. ______________________________
2. ______________________________
3. ______________________________

I lay the following prayers at your feet as I rest in your goodness…

1. ______________________________
2. ______________________________
3. ______________________________

Date ___ / ___ / ___

Therefore, I urge you, brothers and sisters, in view of God's mercy, to offer your bodies as a living sacrifice, holy and pleasing to God —this is your true and proper worship.

-Romans 12:1

Father, I lift up the following in prayer as I start my day…

1. ____________________
2. ____________________
3. ____________________

Father, I am thankful and grateful for….

1. ____________________
2. ____________________
3. ____________________

Today I know you will you give me the strength to….

1. ____________________

I praise you for all your mercies and blessings from today…

1. ____________________
2. ____________________
3. ____________________

I lay the following prayers at your feet as I rest in your goodness…

1. ____________________
2. ____________________
3. ____________________

Date ___ / ___ / ___

In my distress I called to the Lord; I cried to my God for help.
From his temple he heard my voice; my cry came before him, into his ears.

-Psalm 18:6

Father, I lift up the following in prayer as I start my day…

1. ______________________________
2. ______________________________
3. ______________________________

Father, I am thankful and grateful for….

1. ______________________________
2. ______________________________
3. ______________________________

Today I know you will you give me the strength to….

1. ______________________________

I praise you for all your mercies and blessings from today…

1. ______________________________
2. ______________________________
3. ______________________________

I lay the following prayers at your feet as I rest in your goodness…

1. ______________________________
2. ______________________________
3. ______________________________

Date ___ / ___ / ___

But thanks be to God, who always leads us as captives in Christ's triumphal procession and uses us to spread the aroma of the knowledge of him everywhere.

-2 Corinthians 2:14

Father, I lift up the following in prayer as I start my day…

1. ______________________________
2. ______________________________
3. ______________________________

Father, I am thankful and grateful for….

1. ______________________________
2. ______________________________
3. ______________________________

Today I know you will you give me the strength to….

1. ______________________________

I praise you for all your mercies and blessings from today…

1. ______________________________
2. ______________________________
3. ______________________________

I lay the following prayers at your feet as I rest in your goodness…

1. ______________________________
2. ______________________________
3. ______________________________

Date ___ / ___ / ___

By this all men will know that you are my disciples,
if you love one another.

-John 13:35

Father, I lift up the following in prayer as I start my day…

1. ____________________
2. ____________________
3. ____________________

Father, I am thankful and grateful for….

1. ____________________
2. ____________________
3. ____________________

Today I know you will you give me the strength to….

1. ____________________

I praise you for all your mercies and blessings from today…

1. ____________________
2. ____________________
3. ____________________

I lay the following prayers at your feet as I rest in your goodness…

1. ____________________
2. ____________________
3. ____________________

Date ___ / ___ / ___

Restore to me the joy of your salvation
and grant me a willing spirit, to sustain me.

-Psalm 51:12

Father, I lift up the following in prayer as I start my day…

1. ______________________________
2. ______________________________
3. ______________________________

Father, I am thankful and grateful for….

1. ______________________________
2. ______________________________
3. ______________________________

Today I know you will you give me the strength to….

1. ______________________________

I praise you for all your mercies and blessings from today…

1. ______________________________
2. ______________________________
3. ______________________________

I lay the following prayers at your feet as I rest in your goodness…

1. ______________________________
2. ______________________________
3. ______________________________

Date ___ / ___ / ___

Because he himself suffered when he was tempted,
he is able to help those who are being tempted.

-Hebrews 2:18

Father, I lift up the following in prayer as I start my day…

1. ______________________________
2. ______________________________
3. ______________________________

Father, I am thankful and grateful for….

1. ______________________________
2. ______________________________
3. ______________________________

Today I know you will you give me the strength to….

1. ______________________________

I praise you for all your mercies and blessings from today…

1. ______________________________
2. ______________________________
3. ______________________________

I lay the following prayers at your feet as I rest in your goodness…

1. ______________________________
2. ______________________________
3. ______________________________

Date ___ / ___ / ___

Salvation is found in no one else, for there is no other name under heaven given to mankind by which we must be saved.

-Acts 4:12

Father, I lift up the following in prayer as I start my day…

1. ______________________________
2. ______________________________
3. ______________________________

Father, I am thankful and grateful for….

1. ______________________________
2. ______________________________
3. ______________________________

Today I know you will you give me the strength to….

1. ______________________________

I praise you for all your mercies and blessings from today…

1. ______________________________
2. ______________________________
3. ______________________________

I lay the following prayers at your feet as I rest in your goodness…

1. ______________________________
2. ______________________________
3. ______________________________

Date ___ / ___ / ___

Truly he is my rock and my salvation;
he is my fortress, I will not be shaken.

-Psalm 62:6

Father, I lift up the following in prayer as I start my day…

1. ______________________________
2. ______________________________
3. ______________________________

Father, I am thankful and grateful for….

1. ______________________________
2. ______________________________
3. ______________________________

Today I know you will you give me the strength to….

1. ______________________________

I praise you for all your mercies and blessings from today…

1. ______________________________
2. ______________________________
3. ______________________________

I lay the following prayers at your feet as I rest in your goodness…

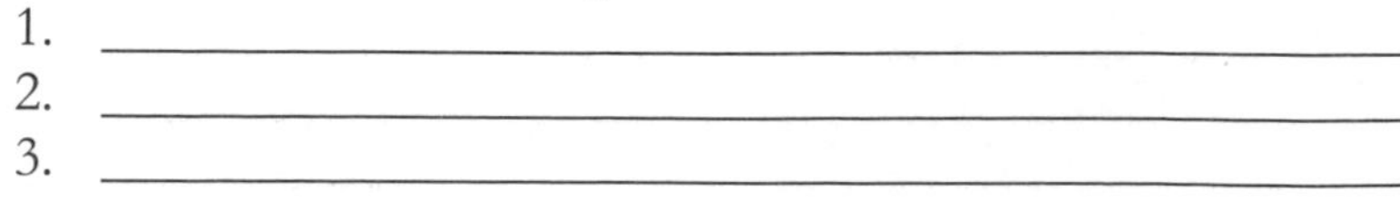

Date ___ / ___ / ___

Devote yourselves to prayer,
being watchful and thankful.

-Colossians 4:2

Father, I lift up the following in prayer as I start my day…

1. ______________________________
2. ______________________________
3. ______________________________

Father, I am thankful and grateful for….

1. ______________________________
2. ______________________________
3. ______________________________

Today I know you will you give me the strength to….

1. ______________________________

I praise you for all your mercies and blessings from today…

1. ______________________________
2. ______________________________
3. ______________________________

I lay the following prayers at your feet as I rest in your goodness…

1. ______________________________
2. ______________________________
3. ______________________________

Date ___ / ___ / ___

Rejoice always, pray continually, give thanks in all circumstances; for this is God's will for you in Christ Jesus.

-1 Thessalonians 5:16-18

Father, I lift up the following in prayer as I start my day…

1. ______________________________
2. ______________________________
3. ______________________________

Father, I am thankful and grateful for….

1. ______________________________
2. ______________________________
3. ______________________________

Today I know you will you give me the strength to….

1. ______________________________

I praise you for all your mercies and blessings from today…

1. ______________________________
2. ______________________________
3. ______________________________

I lay the following prayers at your feet as I rest in your goodness…

1. ______________________________
2. ______________________________
3. ______________________________

Date ___ / ___ / ___

This is how we know what love is: Jesus Christ laid down his life for us. And we ought to lay down our lives for our brothers and sisters.

-1 John 3:16

Father, I lift up the following in prayer as I start my day…

1. ______________________________
2. ______________________________
3. ______________________________

Father, I am thankful and grateful for….

1. ______________________________
2. ______________________________
3. ______________________________

Today I know you will you give me the strength to….

1. ______________________________

I praise you for all your mercies and blessings from today…

1. ______________________________
2. ______________________________
3. ______________________________

I lay the following prayers at your feet as I rest in your goodness…

1. ______________________________
2. ______________________________
3. ______________________________

Date ___ / ___ / ___

No temptation has overtaken you except what is common to mankind. And God is faithful; he will not let you be tempted beyond what you can bear. But when you are tempted, he will also provide a way out so that you can endure it.

_1 Corinthians 10:13

Father, I lift up the following in prayer as I start my day…

1. ______________________________
2. ______________________________
3. ______________________________

Father, I am thankful and grateful for….

1. ______________________________
2. ______________________________
3. ______________________________

Today I know you will you give me the strength to….

1. ______________________________

I praise you for all your mercies and blessings from today…

1. ______________________________
2. ______________________________
3. ______________________________

I lay the following prayers at your feet as I rest in your goodness…

1. ______________________________
2. ______________________________
3. ______________________________

Date ___ / ___ / ___

The LORD is good to those whose hope is in him,
to the one who seeks him;

-Lamentations 3:25

Father, I lift up the following in prayer as I start my day…

1. ______________________________
2. ______________________________
3. ______________________________

Father, I am thankful and grateful for….

1. ______________________________
2. ______________________________
3. ______________________________

Today I know you will you give me the strength to….

1. ______________________________

I praise you for all your mercies and blessings from today…

1. ______________________________
2. ______________________________
3. ______________________________

I lay the following prayers at your feet as I rest in your goodness…

1. ______________________________
2. ______________________________
3. ______________________________

Date ___ / ___ / ___

The LORD is near to all who call on him, to all who call on him in truth. He fulfills the desires of those who fear him; he hears their cry and saves them.

-Psalm 145:18-19

Father, I lift up the following in prayer as I start my day…

1. ______________________________
2. ______________________________
3. ______________________________

Father, I am thankful and grateful for….

1. ______________________________
2. ______________________________
3. ______________________________

Today I know you will you give me the strength to….

1. ______________________________

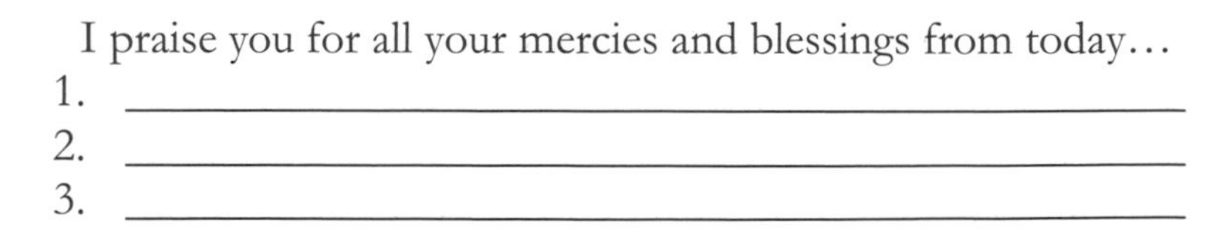

I praise you for all your mercies and blessings from today…

1. ______________________________
2. ______________________________
3. ______________________________

I lay the following prayers at your feet as I rest in your goodness…

1. ______________________________
2. ______________________________
3. ______________________________

Date ___ / ___ / ___

Ask and it will be given to you; seek and you will find; knock and the door will be opened to you. For everyone who asks receives; the one who seeks finds; and to the one who knocks, the door will be opened.

-Luke 11:9-10

Father, I lift up the following in prayer as I start my day…

1. ______________________________
2. ______________________________
3. ______________________________

Father, I am thankful and grateful for….

1. ______________________________
2. ______________________________
3. ______________________________

Today I know you will you give me the strength to….

1. ______________________________

I praise you for all your mercies and blessings from today…

1. ______________________________
2. ______________________________
3. ______________________________

I lay the following prayers at your feet as I rest in your goodness…

1. ______________________________
2. ______________________________
3. ______________________________

Date ___ / ___ / ___

But he said to me, "My grace is sufficient for you, for my power is made perfect in weakness." Therefore I will boast all the more gladly about my weaknesses, so that Christ's power may rest on me.

-2 Corinthians 12:9

Father, I lift up the following in prayer as I start my day…

1. ____________________
2. ____________________
3. ____________________

Father, I am thankful and grateful for….

1. ____________________
2. ____________________
3. ____________________

Today I know you will you give me the strength to….

1. ____________________

I praise you for all your mercies and blessings from today…

1. ____________________
2. ____________________
3. ____________________

I lay the following prayers at your feet as I rest in your goodness…

1. ____________________
2. ____________________
3. ____________________

Date ___ / ___ / ___

Rather, clothe yourselves with the Lord Jesus Christ,
and do not think about how to gratify the desires of the flesh.

-Romans 13:14

Father, I lift up the following in prayer as I start my day…

1. ________________________________
2. ________________________________
3. ________________________________

Father, I am thankful and grateful for….

1. ________________________________
2. ________________________________
3. ________________________________

Today I know you will you give me the strength to….

1. ________________________________

I praise you for all your mercies and blessings from today…

1. ________________________________
2. ________________________________
3. ________________________________

I lay the following prayers at your feet as I rest in your goodness…

1. ________________________________
2. ________________________________
3. ________________________________

Date ___ / ___ / ___

Since you are my rock and my fortress, for the sake of your name lead and guide me.

-Psalm 31:3

Father, I lift up the following in prayer as I start my day…

1. ______________________________
2. ______________________________
3. ______________________________

Father, I am thankful and grateful for….

1. ______________________________
2. ______________________________
3. ______________________________

Today I know you will you give me the strength to….

1. ______________________________

I praise you for all your mercies and blessings from today…

1. ______________________________
2. ______________________________
3. ______________________________

I lay the following prayers at your feet as I rest in your goodness…

1. ______________________________
2. ______________________________
3. ______________________________

Date ___ / ___ / ___

For we live by faith,
not by sight.

-2 Corinthians 5:7

Father, I lift up the following in prayer as I start my day…

1. ______________________________
2. ______________________________
3. ______________________________

Father, I am thankful and grateful for….

1. ______________________________
2. ______________________________
3. ______________________________

Today I know you will you give me the strength to….

1. ______________________________

I praise you for all your mercies and blessings from today…

1. ______________________________
2. ______________________________
3. ______________________________

I lay the following prayers at your feet as I rest in your goodness…

1. ______________________________
2. ______________________________
3. ______________________________

Date ___ / ___ / ___

God, who has called you into fellowship with His Son Jesus Christ our Lord, is faithful.

-1 Corinthians 1:9

Father, I lift up the following in prayer as I start my day…

1. ________________________________
2. ________________________________
3. ________________________________

Father, I am thankful and grateful for….

1. ________________________________
2. ________________________________
3. ________________________________

Today I know you will you give me the strength to….

1. ________________________________

I praise you for all your mercies and blessings from today…

1. ________________________________
2. ________________________________
3. ________________________________

I lay the following prayers at your feet as I rest in your goodness…

1. ________________________________
2. ________________________________
3. ________________________________

Date ___ / ___ / ___

If you declare with your mouth, "Jesus is Lord," and believe in your heart that God raised him from the dead, you will be saved

-Romans 10:9

Father, I lift up the following in prayer as I start my day…

1. ______________________________
2. ______________________________
3. ______________________________

Father, I am thankful and grateful for….

1. ______________________________
2. ______________________________
3. ______________________________

Today I know you will you give me the strength to….

1. ______________________________

I praise you for all your mercies and blessings from today…

1. ______________________________
2. ______________________________
3. ______________________________

I lay the following prayers at your feet as I rest in your goodness…

1. ______________________________
2. ______________________________
3. ______________________________

Date ___ / ___ / ___

God is our refuge and strength, an ever-present help in trouble. Therefore we will not fear, though the earth give way and the mountains fall into the heart of the sea, though its waters roar and the mountains quake with their surging.

-Psalm 46:1-3

Father, I lift up the following in prayer as I start my day…

1. ______________________________
2. ______________________________
3. ______________________________

Father, I am thankful and grateful for….

1. ______________________________
2. ______________________________
3. ______________________________

Today I know you will you give me the strength to….

1. ______________________________

I praise you for all your mercies and blessings from today…

1. ______________________________
2. ______________________________
3. ______________________________

I lay the following prayers at your feet as I rest in your goodness…

1. ______________________________
2. ______________________________
3. ______________________________

Date ___ / ___ / ___

Now to him who is able to do immeasurably more than all we ask or imagine, according to his power that is at work within us, to him be glory in the church and in Christ Jesus throughout all generations, for ever and ever! Amen.

-Ephesians 3:20-21

Father, I lift up the following in prayer as I start my day…

1. ______________________________
2. ______________________________
3. ______________________________

Father, I am thankful and grateful for….

1. ______________________________
2. ______________________________
3. ______________________________

Today I know you will you give me the strength to….

1. ______________________________

I praise you for all your mercies and blessings from today…

1. ______________________________
2. ______________________________
3. ______________________________

I lay the following prayers at your feet as I rest in your goodness…

1. ______________________________
2. ______________________________
3. ______________________________

Date ___ / ___ / ___

Consider it pure joy, my brothers,
whenever you face trials of many kinds,

-James 1:2

Father, I lift up the following in prayer as I start my day…

1. ______________________________
2. ______________________________
3. ______________________________

Father, I am thankful and grateful for….

1. ______________________________
2. ______________________________
3. ______________________________

Today I know you will you give me the strength to….

1. ______________________________

I praise you for all your mercies and blessings from today…

1. ______________________________
2. ______________________________
3. ______________________________

I lay the following prayers at your feet as I rest in your goodness…

1. ______________________________
2. ______________________________
3. ______________________________

Date ___ / ___ / ___

Let us fix our eyes on Jesus, the author and perfecter of our faith, who for the joy set before him endured the cross, scorning its shame, and sat down at the right hand of the throne of God.

-Hebrews 12:2

Father, I lift up the following in prayer as I start my day…

1. ______________________________
2. ______________________________
3. ______________________________

Father, I am thankful and grateful for….

1. ______________________________
2. ______________________________
3. ______________________________

Today I know you will you give me the strength to….

1. ______________________________

I praise you for all your mercies and blessings from today…

1. ______________________________
2. ______________________________
3. ______________________________

I lay the following prayers at your feet as I rest in your goodness…

1. ______________________________
2. ______________________________
3. ______________________________

Date ___ / ___ / ___

But seek first his kingdom and his righteousness,
and all these things will be given to you as well.

-Matthew 6:33

Father, I lift up the following in prayer as I start my day…

1. ______________________________
2. ______________________________
3. ______________________________

Father, I am thankful and grateful for….

1. ______________________________
2. ______________________________
3. ______________________________

Today I know you will you give me the strength to….

1. ______________________________

I praise you for all your mercies and blessings from today…

1. ______________________________
2. ______________________________
3. ______________________________

I lay the following prayers at your feet as I rest in your goodness…

1. ______________________________
2. ______________________________
3. ______________________________

Date ___ / ___ / ___

Know therefore that the LORD your God is God; he is the faithful God, keeping his covenant of love to a thousand generations of those who love him and keep his commandments.

-Deuteronomy 7:9

Father, I lift up the following in prayer as I start my day…

1. ______________________________
2. ______________________________
3. ______________________________

Father, I am thankful and grateful for….

1. ______________________________
2. ______________________________
3. ______________________________

Today I know you will you give me the strength to….

1. ______________________________

I praise you for all your mercies and blessings from today…

1. ______________________________
2. ______________________________
3. ______________________________

I lay the following prayers at your feet as I rest in your goodness…

1. ______________________________
2. ______________________________
3. ______________________________

Date ___ / ___ / ___

The LORD is good, a refuge in times of trouble.
He cares for those who trust in him,

-Nahum 1:7

Father, I lift up the following in prayer as I start my day…

1. ______________________________
2. ______________________________
3. ______________________________

Father, I am thankful and grateful for….

1. ______________________________
2. ______________________________
3. ______________________________

Today I know you will you give me the strength to….

1. ______________________________

I praise you for all your mercies and blessings from today…

1. ______________________________
2. ______________________________
3. ______________________________

I lay the following prayers at your feet as I rest in your goodness…

1. ______________________________
2. ______________________________
3. ______________________________

Date ___ / ___ / ___

But the Lord is faithful, and he will strengthen and protect you from the evil one.

-2 Thessalonians 3:3

Father, I lift up the following in prayer as I start my day…

1. ______________________________
2. ______________________________
3. ______________________________

Father, I am thankful and grateful for….

1. ______________________________
2. ______________________________
3. ______________________________

Today I know you will you give me the strength to….

1. ______________________________

I praise you for all your mercies and blessings from today…

1. ______________________________
2. ______________________________
3. ______________________________

I lay the following prayers at your feet as I rest in your goodness…

1. ______________________________
2. ______________________________
3. ______________________________

Date ___ / ___ / ___

But he was pierced for our transgressions, he was crushed for our iniquities; the punishment that brought us peace was upon him, and by his wounds we are healed.

-Isaiah 53:5

Father, I lift up the following in prayer as I start my day…

1. ____________________
2. ____________________
3. ____________________

Father, I am thankful and grateful for….

1. ____________________
2. ____________________
3. ____________________

Today I know you will you give me the strength to….

1. ____________________

I praise you for all your mercies and blessings from today…

1. ____________________
2. ____________________
3. ____________________

I lay the following prayers at your feet as I rest in your goodness…

1. ____________________
2. ____________________
3. ____________________

Date ___ / ___ / ___

He has showed you, O man, what is good.
And what does the Lord require of you? To act justly and to love mercy and to walk humbly with your God.

-Micah 6:8

Father, I lift up the following in prayer as I start my day…

1. ____________________
2. ____________________
3. ____________________

Father, I am thankful and grateful for….

1. ____________________
2. ____________________
3. ____________________

Today I know you will you give me the strength to….

1. ____________________

I praise you for all your mercies and blessings from today…

1. ____________________
2. ____________________
3. ____________________

I lay the following prayers at your feet as I rest in your goodness…

1. ____________________
2. ____________________
3. ____________________

Date ___ / ___ / ___

Therefore confess your sins to each other and pray for each other so that you may be healed. The prayer of a righteous man is powerful and effective.

-James 5:16

Father, I lift up the following in prayer as I start my day…

1. ______________________________
2. ______________________________
3. ______________________________

Father, I am thankful and grateful for….

1. ______________________________
2. ______________________________
3. ______________________________

Today I know you will you give me the strength to….

1. ______________________________

I praise you for all your mercies and blessings from today…

1. ______________________________
2. ______________________________
3. ______________________________

I lay the following prayers at your feet as I rest in your goodness…

1. ______________________________
2. ______________________________
3. ______________________________

Date ___ / ___ / ___

Do nothing out of selfish ambition or empty pride, but in humility consider others more important than yourselves.

-Philippians 2:3

Father, I lift up the following in prayer as I start my day…

1. ______________________________
2. ______________________________
3. ______________________________

Father, I am thankful and grateful for….

1. ______________________________
2. ______________________________
3. ______________________________

Today I know you will you give me the strength to….

1. ______________________________

I praise you for all your mercies and blessings from today…

1. ______________________________
2. ______________________________
3. ______________________________

I lay the following prayers at your feet as I rest in your goodness…

1. ______________________________
2. ______________________________
3. ______________________________

Date ___ / ___ / ___

I have been crucified with Christ and I no longer live, but Christ lives in me. The life I live in the body, I live by faith in the Son of God, who loved me and gave himself for me.

-Galatians 2:20

Father, I lift up the following in prayer as I start my day…

1. ______________________________
2. ______________________________
3. ______________________________

Father, I am thankful and grateful for….

1. ______________________________
2. ______________________________
3. ______________________________

Today I know you will you give me the strength to….

1. ______________________________

I praise you for all your mercies and blessings from today…

1. ______________________________
2. ______________________________
3. ______________________________

I lay the following prayers at your feet as I rest in your goodness…

1. ______________________________
2. ______________________________
3. ______________________________

Date ___ / ___ / ___

Therefore, as God's chosen people, holy and dearly loved, clothe yourselves with compassion, kindness, humility, gentleness and patience.

-Colossians 3:12

Father, I lift up the following in prayer as I start my day…

1. ______________________________
2. ______________________________
3. ______________________________

Father, I am thankful and grateful for….

1. ______________________________
2. ______________________________
3. ______________________________

Today I know you will you give me the strength to….

1. ______________________________

I praise you for all your mercies and blessings from today…

1. ______________________________
2. ______________________________
3. ______________________________

I lay the following prayers at your feet as I rest in your goodness…

1. ______________________________
2. ______________________________
3. ______________________________

Date ___ / ___ / ___

Cast all your anxiety on him
because he cares for you.

-1 Peter 5:7

Father, I lift up the following in prayer as I start my day…

1. ____
2. ____
3. ____

Father, I am thankful and grateful for….

1. ____
2. ____
3. ____

Today I know you will you give me the strength to….

1. ____

I praise you for all your mercies and blessings from today…

1. ____
2. ____
3. ____

I lay the following prayers at your feet as I rest in your goodness…

1. ____
2. ____
3. ____

Date ___ / ___ / ___

I am convinced that neither death nor life, neither angels nor demons, neither the present nor the future, neither height nor depth, nor anything else in creation, will be able to separate us from the love of God that is in Christ Jesus.

-Romans 8:38-39

Father, I lift up the following in prayer as I start my day…

1. ______________________________
2. ______________________________
3. ______________________________

Father, I am thankful and grateful for….

1. ______________________________
2. ______________________________
3. ______________________________

Today I know you will you give me the strength to….

1. ______________________________

I praise you for all your mercies and blessings from today…

1. ______________________________
2. ______________________________
3. ______________________________

I lay the following prayers at your feet as I rest in your goodness…

1. ______________________________
2. ______________________________
3. ______________________________

Date ___ / ___ / ___

My comfort in my suffering is this:
Your promise preserves my life.

-Psalm 119:50

Father, I lift up the following in prayer as I start my day…

1. ____________________
2. ____________________
3. ____________________

Father, I am thankful and grateful for….

1. ____________________
2. ____________________
3. ____________________

Today I know you will you give me the strength to….

1. ____________________

I praise you for all your mercies and blessings from today…

1. ____________________
2. ____________________
3. ____________________

I lay the following prayers at your feet as I rest in your goodness…

1. ____________________
2. ____________________
3. ____________________

Date ___ / ___ / ___

Jesus replied: "Love the Lord your God with all your heart and with all your soul and with all your mind.'

-Matthew 22:37

Father, I lift up the following in prayer as I start my day…

1. ______________________________
2. ______________________________
3. ______________________________

Father, I am thankful and grateful for….

1. ______________________________
2. ______________________________
3. ______________________________

Today I know you will you give me the strength to….

1. ______________________________

I praise you for all your mercies and blessings from today…

1. ______________________________
2. ______________________________
3. ______________________________

I lay the following prayers at your feet as I rest in your goodness…

1. ______________________________
2. ______________________________
3. ______________________________

Date ___ / ___ / ___

Whatever you do, work at it with all your heart,
as working for the Lord, not for men,

-Colossians 3:23

Father, I lift up the following in prayer as I start my day…

1. ______________________________
2. ______________________________
3. ______________________________

Father, I am thankful and grateful for….

1. ______________________________
2. ______________________________
3. ______________________________

Today I know you will you give me the strength to….

1. ______________________________

I praise you for all your mercies and blessings from today…

1. ______________________________
2. ______________________________
3. ______________________________

I lay the following prayers at your feet as I rest in your goodness…

1. ______________________________
2. ______________________________
3. ______________________________

Date ___ / ___ / ___

Be on your guard; stand firm in the faith;
be courageous; be strong.

-1 Corinthians 16:13

Father, I lift up the following in prayer as I start my day…

1. ______________________________
2. ______________________________
3. ______________________________

Father, I am thankful and grateful for….

1. ______________________________
2. ______________________________
3. ______________________________

Today I know you will you give me the strength to….

1. ______________________________

I praise you for all your mercies and blessings from today…

1. ______________________________
2. ______________________________
3. ______________________________

I lay the following prayers at your feet as I rest in your goodness…

1. ______________________________
2. ______________________________
3. ______________________________

Date ___ / ___ / ___

Praise the Lord, my soul, and forget not all his benefits—who forgives all your sins and heals all your diseases, who redeems your life from the pit and crowns you with love and compassion, who satisfies your desires with good things…

-Psalm 103:2-5

Father, I lift up the following in prayer as I start my day…

1. ______________________________
2. ______________________________
3. ______________________________

Father, I am thankful and grateful for….

1. ______________________________
2. ______________________________
3. ______________________________

Today I know you will you give me the strength to….

1. ______________________________

I praise you for all your mercies and blessings from today…

1. ______________________________
2. ______________________________
3. ______________________________

I lay the following prayers at your feet as I rest in your goodness…

1. ______________________________
2. ______________________________
3. ______________________________

Date ___ / ___ / ___

For we do not have a high priest who is unable to sympathize with our weaknesses, but we have one who has been tempted in every way, just as we are—yet was without sin.

-Hebrews 4:15

Father, I lift up the following in prayer as I start my day…

1. ______________________________
2. ______________________________
3. ______________________________

Father, I am thankful and grateful for….

1. ______________________________
2. ______________________________
3. ______________________________

Today I know you will you give me the strength to….

1. ______________________________

I praise you for all your mercies and blessings from today…

1. ______________________________
2. ______________________________
3. ______________________________

I lay the following prayers at your feet as I rest in your goodness…

1. ______________________________
2. ______________________________
3. ______________________________

Date ___ / ___ / ___

May the God of hope fill you with all joy and peace as you trust in him, so that you may overflow with hope by the power of the Holy Spirit.

-Romans 15:13

Father, I lift up the following in prayer as I start my day…

1. ______________________________
2. ______________________________
3. ______________________________

Father, I am thankful and grateful for….

1. ______________________________
2. ______________________________
3. ______________________________

Today I know you will you give me the strength to….

1. ______________________________

I praise you for all your mercies and blessings from today…

1. ______________________________
2. ______________________________
3. ______________________________

I lay the following prayers at your feet as I rest in your goodness…

1. ______________________________
2. ______________________________
3. ______________________________

Date ___ / ___ / ___

What, then, shall we say in response to these things?
If God is for us, who can be against us?

-Romans 8:31

Father, I lift up the following in prayer as I start my day…

1. ______________________________
2. ______________________________
3. ______________________________

Father, I am thankful and grateful for….

1. ______________________________
2. ______________________________
3. ______________________________

Today I know you will you give me the strength to….

1. ______________________________

I praise you for all your mercies and blessings from today…

1. ______________________________
2. ______________________________
3. ______________________________

I lay the following prayers at your feet as I rest in your goodness…

1. ______________________________
2. ______________________________
3. ______________________________

Date ___ / ___ / ___

I can do everything through him who gives me strength.

-Philippians 4:13

Father, I lift up the following in prayer as I start my day…

1. ______________________________
2. ______________________________
3. ______________________________

Father, I am thankful and grateful for….

1. ______________________________
2. ______________________________
3. ______________________________

Today I know you will you give me the strength to….

1. ______________________________

I praise you for all your mercies and blessings from today…

1. ______________________________
2. ______________________________
3. ______________________________

I lay the following prayers at your feet as I rest in your goodness…

1. ______________________________
2. ______________________________
3. ______________________________

Date ___ / ___ / ___

For everything that was written in the past was written to teach us, so that through the endurance taught in the Scriptures and the encouragement they provide we might have hope.

-Romans 15:4

Father, I lift up the following in prayer as I start my day…

1. ______________________________
2. ______________________________
3. ______________________________

Father, I am thankful and grateful for….

1. ______________________________
2. ______________________________
3. ______________________________

Today I know you will you give me the strength to….

1. ______________________________

I praise you for all your mercies and blessings from today…

1. ______________________________
2. ______________________________
3. ______________________________

I lay the following prayers at your feet as I rest in your goodness…

1. ______________________________
2. ______________________________
3. ______________________________

Date ___ / ___ / ___

I will instruct you and teach you in the way you should go;
I will counsel you with my loving eye on you.

-Psalm 32:8

Father, I lift up the following in prayer as I start my day…

1. ______________________________
2. ______________________________
3. ______________________________

Father, I am thankful and grateful for….

1. ______________________________
2. ______________________________
3. ______________________________

Today I know you will you give me the strength to….

1. ______________________________

I praise you for all your mercies and blessings from today…

1. ______________________________
2. ______________________________
3. ______________________________

I lay the following prayers at your feet as I rest in your goodness…

1. ______________________________
2. ______________________________
3. ______________________________

Date ___ / ___ / ___

Taste and see that the LORD is good;
blessed is the one who takes refuge in him.

-Psalm 34:8

Father, I lift up the following in prayer as I start my day…

1. ______________________________
2. ______________________________
3. ______________________________

Father, I am thankful and grateful for….

1. ______________________________
2. ______________________________
3. ______________________________

Today I know you will you give me the strength to….

1. ______________________________

I praise you for all your mercies and blessings from today…

1. ______________________________
2. ______________________________
3. ______________________________

I lay the following prayers at your feet as I rest in your goodness…

1. ______________________________
2. ______________________________
3. ______________________________

Date ___ / ___ / ___

Jesus answered, "I am the way and the truth and the life. No one comes to the Father except through me.

-John 14:6

Father, I lift up the following in prayer as I start my day…

1. ______________________________
2. ______________________________
3. ______________________________

Father, I am thankful and grateful for….

1. ______________________________
2. ______________________________
3. ______________________________

Today I know you will you give me the strength to….

1. ______________________________

I praise you for all your mercies and blessings from today…

1. ______________________________
2. ______________________________
3. ______________________________

I lay the following prayers at your feet as I rest in your goodness…

1. ______________________________
2. ______________________________
3. ______________________________

Date ___ / ___ / ___

The Lord himself goes before you and will be with you; he will never leave you nor forsake you. Do not be afraid; do not be discouraged.

-Deuteronomy 31:8

Father, I lift up the following in prayer as I start my day…

1. ______________________________
2. ______________________________
3. ______________________________

Father, I am thankful and grateful for….

1. ______________________________
2. ______________________________
3. ______________________________

Today I know you will you give me the strength to….

1. ______________________________

I praise you for all your mercies and blessings from today…

1. ______________________________
2. ______________________________
3. ______________________________

I lay the following prayers at your feet as I rest in your goodness…

1. ______________________________
2. ______________________________
3. ______________________________

Date ___ / ___ / ___

For I am the Lord your God who takes hold of your right hand and says to you, Do not fear; I will help you.

-Isaiah 41:13

Father, I lift up the following in prayer as I start my day…

1. ______________________________
2. ______________________________
3. ______________________________

Father, I am thankful and grateful for….

1. ______________________________
2. ______________________________
3. ______________________________

Today I know you will you give me the strength to….

1. ______________________________

I praise you for all your mercies and blessings from today…

1. ______________________________
2. ______________________________
3. ______________________________

I lay the following prayers at your feet as I rest in your goodness…

1. ______________________________
2. ______________________________
3. ______________________________

Date ___ / ___ / ___

Father, I want those you have given me to be with me where I am, and to see my glory, the glory you have given me because you loved me before the creation of the world.

-John 17:24

Father, I lift up the following in prayer as I start my day…

1. ______________________________
2. ______________________________
3. ______________________________

Father, I am thankful and grateful for….

1. ______________________________
2. ______________________________
3. ______________________________

Today I know you will you give me the strength to….

1. ______________________________

I praise you for all your mercies and blessings from today…

1. ______________________________
2. ______________________________
3. ______________________________

I lay the following prayers at your feet as I rest in your goodness…

1. ______________________________
2. ______________________________
3. ______________________________

Date ___ / ___ / ___

Then you will call on me and come and pray to me,
and I will listen to you.

-Jeremiah 29:12

Father, I lift up the following in prayer as I start my day…

1. ______________________________
2. ______________________________
3. ______________________________

Father, I am thankful and grateful for….

1. ______________________________
2. ______________________________
3. ______________________________

Today I know you will you give me the strength to….

1. ______________________________

I praise you for all your mercies and blessings from today…

1. ______________________________
2. ______________________________
3. ______________________________

I lay the following prayers at your feet as I rest in your goodness…

1. ______________________________
2. ______________________________
3. ______________________________

Date ___ / ___ / ___

You are my refuge and my shield; I have put my hope in your word. Away from me, you evildoers, that I may keep the commands of my God!

-Psalm 119:114-115

Father, I lift up the following in prayer as I start my day…

1. ______________________________
2. ______________________________
3. ______________________________

Father, I am thankful and grateful for….

1. ______________________________
2. ______________________________
3. ______________________________

Today I know you will you give me the strength to….

1. ______________________________

I praise you for all your mercies and blessings from today…

1. ______________________________
2. ______________________________
3. ______________________________

I lay the following prayers at your feet as I rest in your goodness…

1. ______________________________
2. ______________________________
3. ______________________________

Date ___ / ___ / ___

Call to me and I will answer you and tell you great and unsearchable things you do not know.

-Jeremiah 33:3

Father, I lift up the following in prayer as I start my day…

1. ______________________________
2. ______________________________
3. ______________________________

Father, I am thankful and grateful for….

1. ______________________________
2. ______________________________
3. ______________________________

Today I know you will you give me the strength to….

1. ______________________________

I praise you for all your mercies and blessings from today…

1. ______________________________
2. ______________________________
3. ______________________________

I lay the following prayers at your feet as I rest in your goodness…

1. ______________________________
2. ______________________________
3. ______________________________

Date ___ / ___ / ___

The righteous person may have many troubles,
but the LORD delivers him from them all;

-Psalm 34:19

Father, I lift up the following in prayer as I start my day…

1. ______________________________
2. ______________________________
3. ______________________________

Father, I am thankful and grateful for….

1. ______________________________
2. ______________________________
3. ______________________________

Today I know you will you give me the strength to….

1. ______________________________

I praise you for all your mercies and blessings from today…

1. ______________________________
2. ______________________________
3. ______________________________

I lay the following prayers at your feet as I rest in your goodness…

1. ______________________________
2. ______________________________
3. ______________________________

Date ___ / ___ / ___

Now faith is being sure of what we hope for and certain of what we do not see.

-Hebrews 11:1

Father, I lift up the following in prayer as I start my day…

1. ______________________________
2. ______________________________
3. ______________________________

Father, I am thankful and grateful for….

1. ______________________________
2. ______________________________
3. ______________________________

Today I know you will you give me the strength to….

1. ______________________________

I praise you for all your mercies and blessings from today…

1. ______________________________
2. ______________________________
3. ______________________________

I lay the following prayers at your feet as I rest in your goodness…

1. ______________________________
2. ______________________________
3. ______________________________

Date ___ / ___ / ___

And we know that in all things God works for the good of those who love him, who have been called according to his purpose.

-Romans 8:28

Father, I lift up the following in prayer as I start my day…

1. ______________________________
2. ______________________________
3. ______________________________

Father, I am thankful and grateful for….

1. ______________________________
2. ______________________________
3. ______________________________

Today I know you will you give me the strength to….

1. ______________________________

I praise you for all your mercies and blessings from today…

1. ______________________________
2. ______________________________
3. ______________________________

I lay the following prayers at your feet as I rest in your goodness…

1. ______________________________
2. ______________________________
3. ______________________________

Date ___ / ___ / ___

Have I not commanded you? Be strong and courageous. Do not be afraid; do not be discouraged, for the Lord your God will be with you wherever you go.

-Joshua 1:9

Father, I lift up the following in prayer as I start my day…

1. ______________________________
2. ______________________________
3. ______________________________

Father, I am thankful and grateful for….

1. ______________________________
2. ______________________________
3. ______________________________

Today I know you will you give me the strength to….

1. ______________________________

I praise you for all your mercies and blessings from today…

1. ______________________________
2. ______________________________
3. ______________________________

I lay the following prayers at your feet as I rest in your goodness…

1. ______________________________
2. ______________________________
3. ______________________________

Date ___ / ___ / ___

…in all your ways acknowledge him,
and he will make your paths straight

-Proverbs 3:6

Father, I lift up the following in prayer as I start my day…

1. ______________________________
2. ______________________________
3. ______________________________

Father, I am thankful and grateful for….

1. ______________________________
2. ______________________________
3. ______________________________

Today I know you will you give me the strength to….

1. ______________________________

I praise you for all your mercies and blessings from today…

1. ______________________________
2. ______________________________
3. ______________________________

I lay the following prayers at your feet as I rest in your goodness…

1. ______________________________
2. ______________________________
3. ______________________________

Date ___ / ___ / ___

Therefore, since we are surrounded by such a great cloud of witnesses,
let us throw off everything that hinders and the sin that so easily entangles,
and let us run with perseverance the race marked out for us.

-Hebrews 12:1

Father, I lift up the following in prayer as I start my day…

1. ____________________
2. ____________________
3. ____________________

Father, I am thankful and grateful for….

1. ____________________
2. ____________________
3. ____________________

Today I know you will you give me the strength to….

1. ____________________

I praise you for all your mercies and blessings from today…

1. ____________________
2. ____________________
3. ____________________

I lay the following prayers at your feet as I rest in your goodness…

1. ____________________
2. ____________________
3. ____________________

Date ___ / ___ / ___

In the morning, Lord, you hear my voice; in the morning I lay my requests before you and wait expectantly.

-Psalm 5:3

Father, I lift up the following in prayer as I start my day…

1. ______________________________
2. ______________________________
3. ______________________________

Father, I am thankful and grateful for….

1. ______________________________
2. ______________________________
3. ______________________________

Today I know you will you give me the strength to….

1. ______________________________

I praise you for all your mercies and blessings from today…

1. ______________________________
2. ______________________________
3. ______________________________

I lay the following prayers at your feet as I rest in your goodness…

1. ______________________________
2. ______________________________
3. ______________________________

Date ___ / ___ / ___

Let us then approach God's throne of grace with confidence,
so that we may receive mercy and find grace to help us in our time of need.

-Hebrews 4:16

Father, I lift up the following in prayer as I start my day…

1. ______________________________
2. ______________________________
3. ______________________________

Father, I am thankful and grateful for….

1. ______________________________
2. ______________________________
3. ______________________________

Today I know you will you give me the strength to….

1. ______________________________

I praise you for all your mercies and blessings from today…

1. ______________________________
2. ______________________________
3. ______________________________

I lay the following prayers at your feet as I rest in your goodness…

1. ______________________________
2. ______________________________
3. ______________________________

Date ___ / ___ / ___

For the word of God is living and active. Sharper than any double-edged sword, it penetrates even to dividing soul and spirit, joints and marrow; it judges the thoughts and attitudes of the heart.

-Hebrews 4:12

Father, I lift up the following in prayer as I start my day…

1. ______________________________
2. ______________________________
3. ______________________________

Father, I am thankful and grateful for….

1. ______________________________
2. ______________________________
3. ______________________________

Today I know you will you give me the strength to….

1. ______________________________

I praise you for all your mercies and blessings from today…

1. ______________________________
2. ______________________________
3. ______________________________

I lay the following prayers at your feet as I rest in your goodness…

1. ______________________________
2. ______________________________
3. ______________________________

Date ___ / ___ / ___

Do not be anxious about anything, but in everything,
by prayer and petition, with thanksgiving, present your requests to God.

-Philippians 4:6

Father, I lift up the following in prayer as I start my day…

1. ____________________
2. ____________________
3. ____________________

Father, I am thankful and grateful for….

1. ____________________
2. ____________________
3. ____________________

Today I know you will you give me the strength to….

1. ____________________

I praise you for all your mercies and blessings from today…

1. ____________________
2. ____________________
3. ____________________

I lay the following prayers at your feet as I rest in your goodness…

1. ____________________
2. ____________________
3. ____________________

Date ___ / ___ / ___

He himself bore our sins in his body on the cross,
so that we might die to sins and live for righteousness;
by his wounds you have been healed.

-1 Peter 2:24

Father, I lift up the following in prayer as I start my day…

1. ______________________________
2. ______________________________
3. ______________________________

Father, I am thankful and grateful for….

1. ______________________________
2. ______________________________
3. ______________________________

Today I know you will you give me the strength to….

1. ______________________________

I praise you for all your mercies and blessings from today…

1. ______________________________
2. ______________________________
3. ______________________________

I lay the following prayers at your feet as I rest in your goodness…

1. ______________________________
2. ______________________________
3. ______________________________

Date ___ / ___ / ___

But when you pray, go into your room, close the door and pray to your Father, who is unseen. Then your Father, who sees what is done in secret, will reward you.

-Matthew 6:6

Father, I lift up the following in prayer as I start my day…

1. ____________________
2. ____________________
3. ____________________

Father, I am thankful and grateful for….

1. ____________________
2. ____________________
3. ____________________

Today I know you will you give me the strength to….

1. ____________________

I praise you for all your mercies and blessings from today…

1. ____________________
2. ____________________
3. ____________________

I lay the following prayers at your feet as I rest in your goodness…

1. ____________________
2. ____________________
3. ____________________

Date ___ / ___ / ___

Joshua said to them, "Do not be afraid; do not be discouraged. Be strong and courageous. This is what the Lord will do to all the enemies you are going to fight."

-Joshua 10:25

Father, I lift up the following in prayer as I start my day…

1. ______________________
2. ______________________
3. ______________________

Father, I am thankful and grateful for….

1. ______________________
2. ______________________
3. ______________________

Today I know you will you give me the strength to….

1. ______________________

I praise you for all your mercies and blessings from today…

1. ______________________
2. ______________________
3. ______________________

I lay the following prayers at your feet as I rest in your goodness…

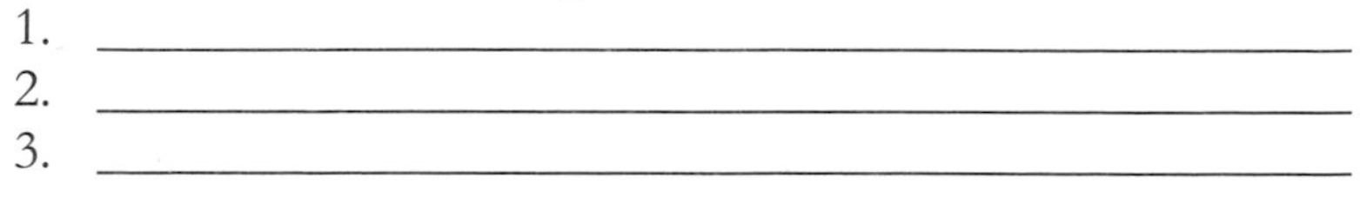

1. ______________________
2. ______________________
3. ______________________

Date ___ / ___ / ___

We all, like sheep, have gone astray, each of us has turned to his own way; and the Lord has laid on him the iniquity of us all.

-Isaiah 53:6

Father, I lift up the following in prayer as I start my day…

1. ____________________
2. ____________________
3. ____________________

Father, I am thankful and grateful for….

1. ____________________
2. ____________________
3. ____________________

Today I know you will you give me the strength to….

1. ____________________

I praise you for all your mercies and blessings from today…

1. ____________________
2. ____________________
3. ____________________

I lay the following prayers at your feet as I rest in your goodness…

1. ____________________
2. ____________________
3. ____________________

Date ___ / ___ / ___

Ask and it will be given to you; seek and you will find; knock and the door will be opened to you. For everyone who asks receives; the one who seeks finds; and to the one who knocks, the door will be opened.

-Matthew 7:7-8

Father, I lift up the following in prayer as I start my day…

1. ______________________________
2. ______________________________
3. ______________________________

Father, I am thankful and grateful for….

1. ______________________________
2. ______________________________
3. ______________________________

Today I know you will you give me the strength to….

1. ______________________________

I praise you for all your mercies and blessings from today…

1. ______________________________
2. ______________________________
3. ______________________________

I lay the following prayers at your feet as I rest in your goodness…

1. ______________________________
2. ______________________________
3. ______________________________

Date ___ / ___ / ___

They devoted themselves to the apostles' teaching and to fellowship, to the breaking of bread and to prayer.

-Acts 2:42

Father, I lift up the following in prayer as I start my day…

1. ______________________________
2. ______________________________
3. ______________________________

Father, I am thankful and grateful for….

1. ______________________________
2. ______________________________
3. ______________________________

Today I know you will you give me the strength to….

1. ______________________________

I praise you for all your mercies and blessings from today…

1. ______________________________
2. ______________________________
3. ______________________________

I lay the following prayers at your feet as I rest in your goodness…

1. ______________________________
2. ______________________________
3. ______________________________

Date ___ / ___ / ___

Remain in me, as I also remain in you.
No branch can bear fruit by itself; it must remain in the vine.
Neither can you bear fruit unless you remain in me.

-John 15:4

Father, I lift up the following in prayer as I start my day…

1. ______________________________
2. ______________________________
3. ______________________________

Father, I am thankful and grateful for….

1. ______________________________
2. ______________________________
3. ______________________________

Today I know you will you give me the strength to….

1. ______________________________

I praise you for all your mercies and blessings from today…

1. ______________________________
2. ______________________________
3. ______________________________

I lay the following prayers at your feet as I rest in your goodness…

1. ______________________________
2. ______________________________
3. ______________________________

Date ___ / ___ / ___

But thanks be to God! He gives us the victory through our Lord Jesus Christ.

-1 Corinthians 15:57

Father, I lift up the following in prayer as I start my day…

1. ______________________________
2. ______________________________
3. ______________________________

Father, I am thankful and grateful for….

1. ______________________________
2. ______________________________
3. ______________________________

Today I know you will you give me the strength to….

1. ______________________________

I praise you for all your mercies and blessings from today…

1. ______________________________
2. ______________________________
3. ______________________________

I lay the following prayers at your feet as I rest in your goodness…

1. ______________________________
2. ______________________________
3. ______________________________

Date ___ / ___ / ___

"For I know the plans I have for you," declares the Lord, "plans to prosper you and not to harm you, plans to give you hope and a future."

-Jeremiah 29:11

Father, I lift up the following in prayer as I start my day…

1. ______________________________
2. ______________________________
3. ______________________________

Father, I am thankful and grateful for….

1. ______________________________
2. ______________________________
3. ______________________________

Today I know you will you give me the strength to….

1. ______________________________

I praise you for all your mercies and blessings from today…

1. ______________________________
2. ______________________________
3. ______________________________

I lay the following prayers at your feet as I rest in your goodness…

1. ______________________________
2. ______________________________
3. ______________________________

Date ___ / ___ / ___

I keep my eyes always on the Lord.
With him at my right hand, I will not be shaken.

-Psalm 16:8

Father, I lift up the following in prayer as I start my day…

1. ______________________________
2. ______________________________
3. ______________________________

Father, I am thankful and grateful for….

1. ______________________________
2. ______________________________
3. ______________________________

Today I know you will you give me the strength to….

1. ______________________________

I praise you for all your mercies and blessings from today…

1. ______________________________
2. ______________________________
3. ______________________________

I lay the following prayers at your feet as I rest in your goodness…

1. ______________________________
2. ______________________________
3. ______________________________

Date ___ / ___ / ___

Keep your lives free from the love of money and be content with what you have, because God has said, "Never will I leave you; never will I forsake you."

-Hebrews 13:5

Father, I lift up the following in prayer as I start my day…

1. ______________________________
2. ______________________________
3. ______________________________

Father, I am thankful and grateful for….

1. ______________________________
2. ______________________________
3. ______________________________

Today I know you will you give me the strength to….

1. ______________________________

I praise you for all your mercies and blessings from today…

1. ______________________________
2. ______________________________
3. ______________________________

I lay the following prayers at your feet as I rest in your goodness…

1. ______________________________
2. ______________________________
3. ______________________________

Date ___ / ___ / ___

The Lord is a refuge for the oppressed,
a stronghold in times of trouble.

-Psalm 9:9

Father, I lift up the following in prayer as I start my day…

1. ______________________________
2. ______________________________
3. ______________________________

Father, I am thankful and grateful for….

1. ______________________________
2. ______________________________
3. ______________________________

Today I know you will you give me the strength to….

1. ______________________________

I praise you for all your mercies and blessings from today…

1. ______________________________
2. ______________________________
3. ______________________________

I lay the following prayers at your feet as I rest in your goodness…

1. ______________________________
2. ______________________________
3. ______________________________

Date ___ / ___ / ___

God made him who had no sin to be sin for us,
so that in him we might become the righteousness of God.

-2 Corinthians 5:21

Father, I lift up the following in prayer as I start my day…

1. ______________________________
2. ______________________________
3. ______________________________

Father, I am thankful and grateful for….

1. ______________________________
2. ______________________________
3. ______________________________

Today I know you will you give me the strength to….

1. ______________________________

I praise you for all your mercies and blessings from today…

1. ______________________________
2. ______________________________
3. ______________________________

I lay the following prayers at your feet as I rest in your goodness…

1. ______________________________
2. ______________________________
3. ______________________________

Date ___ / ___ / ___

A generous person will prosper;
whoever refreshes others will be refreshed.

-Proverbs 11:25

Father, I lift up the following in prayer as I start my day…

1. ______________________________
2. ______________________________
3. ______________________________

Father, I am thankful and grateful for….

1. ______________________________
2. ______________________________
3. ______________________________

Today I know you will you give me the strength to….

1. ______________________________

I praise you for all your mercies and blessings from today…

1. ______________________________
2. ______________________________
3. ______________________________

I lay the following prayers at your feet as I rest in your goodness…

1. ______________________________
2. ______________________________
3. ______________________________

Date ___ / ___ / ___

But I tell you, love your enemies
and pray for those who persecute you.

-Matthew 5:44

Father, I lift up the following in prayer as I start my day…

1. ______________________________
2. ______________________________
3. ______________________________

Father, I am thankful and grateful for….

1. ______________________________
2. ______________________________
3. ______________________________

Today I know you will you give me the strength to….

1. ______________________________

I praise you for all your mercies and blessings from today…

1. ______________________________
2. ______________________________
3. ______________________________

I lay the following prayers at your feet as I rest in your goodness…

1. ______________________________
2. ______________________________
3. ______________________________

Date ___ / ___ / ___

Finally, be strong in the Lord and in his mighty power.
Put on the full armor of God, so that you can
take your stand against the devil's schemes.

-Ephesians 6:10-11

Father, I lift up the following in prayer as I start my day…

1. ______________________________
2. ______________________________
3. ______________________________

Father, I am thankful and grateful for….

1. ______________________________
2. ______________________________
3. ______________________________

Today I know you will you give me the strength to….

1. ______________________________

I praise you for all your mercies and blessings from today…

1. ______________________________
2. ______________________________
3. ______________________________

I lay the following prayers at your feet as I rest in your goodness…

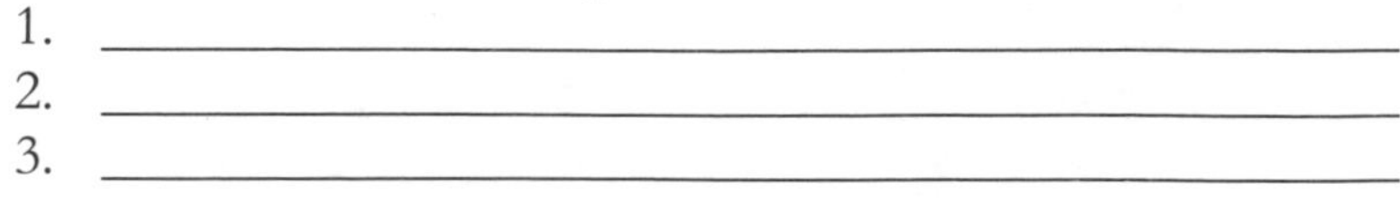

1. ______________________________
2. ______________________________
3. ______________________________

Date ___ / ___ / ___

Greater love has no one than this,
that he lay down his life for his friends.

-John 15:13

Father, I lift up the following in prayer as I start my day…

1. ______________________________
2. ______________________________
3. ______________________________

Father, I am thankful and grateful for….

1. ______________________________
2. ______________________________
3. ______________________________

Today I know you will you give me the strength to….

1. ______________________________

I praise you for all your mercies and blessings from today…

1. ______________________________
2. ______________________________
3. ______________________________

I lay the following prayers at your feet as I rest in your goodness…

1. ______________________________
2. ______________________________
3. ______________________________

Date ___ / ___ / ___

May these words of my mouth and this meditation of my heart be pleasing in your sight, Lord, my Rock and my Redeemer.

-Psalm 19:14

Father, I lift up the following in prayer as I start my day…

1. ______________________________
2. ______________________________
3. ______________________________

Father, I am thankful and grateful for….

1. ______________________________
2. ______________________________
3. ______________________________

Today I know you will you give me the strength to….

1. ______________________________

I praise you for all your mercies and blessings from today…

1. ______________________________
2. ______________________________
3. ______________________________

I lay the following prayers at your feet as I rest in your goodness…

1. ______________________________
2. ______________________________
3. ______________________________

Date ___ / ___ / ___

And when you stand praying, if you hold anything against anyone, forgive them, so that your Father in heaven may forgive you your sins.

-Mark 11:25

Father, I lift up the following in prayer as I start my day…

1. ______________________________
2. ______________________________
3. ______________________________

Father, I am thankful and grateful for….

1. ______________________________
2. ______________________________
3. ______________________________

Today I know you will you give me the strength to….

1. ______________________________

I praise you for all your mercies and blessings from today…

1. ______________________________
2. ______________________________
3. ______________________________

I lay the following prayers at your feet as I rest in your goodness…

1. ______________________________
2. ______________________________
3. ______________________________

Date ___ / ___ / ___

For the eyes of the Lord are on the righteous and his ears are attentive to their prayer, but the face of the Lord is against those who do evil.

-1 Peter 3:12

Father, I lift up the following in prayer as I start my day…

1. ______________________________
2. ______________________________
3. ______________________________

Father, I am thankful and grateful for….

1. ______________________________
2. ______________________________
3. ______________________________

Today I know you will you give me the strength to….

1. ______________________________

I praise you for all your mercies and blessings from today…

1. ______________________________
2. ______________________________
3. ______________________________

I lay the following prayers at your feet as I rest in your goodness…

1. ______________________________
2. ______________________________
3. ______________________________

Date ___ / ___ / ___

The Lord will rescue me from every evil attack and will bring me safely to his heavenly kingdom. To him be glory for ever and ever. Amen.

-2 Timothy 4:18

Father, I lift up the following in prayer as I start my day…

1. ______________________________
2. ______________________________
3. ______________________________

Father, I am thankful and grateful for….

1. ______________________________
2. ______________________________
3. ______________________________

Today I know you will you give me the strength to….

1. ______________________________

I praise you for all your mercies and blessings from today…

1. ______________________________
2. ______________________________
3. ______________________________

I lay the following prayers at your feet as I rest in your goodness…

1. ______________________________
2. ______________________________
3. ______________________________

Date ___ / ___ / ___

Be kind and tender-hearted to one another,
forgiving each other just as in Christ God forgave you.

-Ephesians 4:32

Father, I lift up the following in prayer as I start my day…

1. ______________________________
2. ______________________________
3. ______________________________

Father, I am thankful and grateful for….

1. ______________________________
2. ______________________________
3. ______________________________

Today I know you will you give me the strength to….

1. ______________________________

I praise you for all your mercies and blessings from today…

1. ______________________________
2. ______________________________
3. ______________________________

I lay the following prayers at your feet as I rest in your goodness…

1. ______________________________
2. ______________________________
3. ______________________________

Date ___ / ___ / ___

For it is by grace you have been saved, through faith
—and this not from yourselves, it is the gift of God—
not by works, so that no one can boast.

-Ephesians 2:8-9

Father, I lift up the following in prayer as I start my day…

1. ______________________________
2. ______________________________
3. ______________________________

Father, I am thankful and grateful for….

1. ______________________________
2. ______________________________
3. ______________________________

Today I know you will you give me the strength to….

1. ______________________________

I praise you for all your mercies and blessings from today…

1. ______________________________
2. ______________________________
3. ______________________________

I lay the following prayers at your feet as I rest in your goodness…

1. ______________________________
2. ______________________________
3. ______________________________

Date ___ / ___ / ___

For God so loved the world that he gave his one and only Son,
that whoever believes in him shall not perish but have eternal life.

-John 3:16

Father, I lift up the following in prayer as I start my day…

1. ______________________________
2. ______________________________
3. ______________________________

Father, I am thankful and grateful for….

1. ______________________________
2. ______________________________
3. ______________________________

Today I know you will you give me the strength to….

1. ______________________________

I praise you for all your mercies and blessings from today…

1. ______________________________
2. ______________________________
3. ______________________________

I lay the following prayers at your feet as I rest in your goodness…

1. ______________________________
2. ______________________________
3. ______________________________

Date ___ / ___ / ___

Therefore I tell you, whatever you ask for in prayer, believe that you have received it, and it will be yours.

-Mark 11:24

Father, I lift up the following in prayer as I start my day…

1. ______________________________
2. ______________________________
3. ______________________________

Father, I am thankful and grateful for….

1. ______________________________
2. ______________________________
3. ______________________________

Today I know you will you give me the strength to….

1. ______________________________

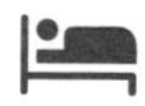

I praise you for all your mercies and blessings from today…

1. ______________________________
2. ______________________________
3. ______________________________

I lay the following prayers at your feet as I rest in your goodness…

1. ______________________________
2. ______________________________
3. ______________________________

Date ___ / ___ / ___

When hard pressed, I cried to the Lord;
he brought me into a spacious place.

-Psalm 118:5

Father, I lift up the following in prayer as I start my day…

1. ______________________________
2. ______________________________
3. ______________________________

Father, I am thankful and grateful for….

1. ______________________________
2. ______________________________
3. ______________________________

Today I know you will you give me the strength to….

1. ______________________________

I praise you for all your mercies and blessings from today…

1. ______________________________
2. ______________________________
3. ______________________________

I lay the following prayers at your feet as I rest in your goodness…

1. ______________________________
2. ______________________________
3. ______________________________

Date ___ / ___ / ___

Trust in the Lord with all your heart
and lean not on your own understanding

-Proverbs 3:5

Father, I lift up the following in prayer as I start my day…

1. ______________________________
2. ______________________________
3. ______________________________

Father, I am thankful and grateful for….

1. ______________________________
2. ______________________________
3. ______________________________

Today I know you will you give me the strength to….

1. ______________________________

I praise you for all your mercies and blessings from today…

1. ______________________________
2. ______________________________
3. ______________________________

I lay the following prayers at your feet as I rest in your goodness…

1. ______________________________
2. ______________________________
3. ______________________________

Date ___ / ___ / ___

Come to me, all you who are weary and burdened,
and I will give you rest.

-Matthew 11:28

Father, I lift up the following in prayer as I start my day…

1. ______________________________
2. ______________________________
3. ______________________________

Father, I am thankful and grateful for….

1. ______________________________
2. ______________________________
3. ______________________________

Today I know you will you give me the strength to….

1. ______________________________

I praise you for all your mercies and blessings from today…

1. ______________________________
2. ______________________________
3. ______________________________

I lay the following prayers at your feet as I rest in your goodness…

1. ______________________________
2. ______________________________
3. ______________________________

Date ___ / ___ / ___

…being confident of this, that he who began a good work in you will carry it on to completion until the day of Christ Jesus.

-Philippians 1:6

Father, I lift up the following in prayer as I start my day…

1. ______
2. ______
3. ______

Father, I am thankful and grateful for….

1. ______
2. ______
3. ______

Today I know you will you give me the strength to….

1. ______

I praise you for all your mercies and blessings from today…

1. ______
2. ______
3. ______

I lay the following prayers at your feet as I rest in your goodness…

1. ______
2. ______
3. ______

Date ___ / ___ / ___

For we are God's workmanship, created in Christ Jesus to do good works, which God prepared in advance for us to do.

-Ephesians 2:10

Father, I lift up the following in prayer as I start my day…

1. ______________________________
2. ______________________________
3. ______________________________

Father, I am thankful and grateful for….

1. ______________________________
2. ______________________________
3. ______________________________

Today I know you will you give me the strength to….

1. ______________________________

I praise you for all your mercies and blessings from today…

1. ______________________________
2. ______________________________
3. ______________________________

I lay the following prayers at your feet as I rest in your goodness…

1. ______________________________
2. ______________________________
3. ______________________________

Date ___ / ___ / ___

So that Christ may dwell in your hearts through faith. And I pray that you, being rooted and established in love, may have power, together with all the Lord's holy people, to grasp how wide, long, high and deep is the love of Christ

-Ephesians 3:17-18

Father, I lift up the following in prayer as I start my day…

1. ______________________________
2. ______________________________
3. ______________________________

Father, I am thankful and grateful for….

1. ______________________________
2. ______________________________
3. ______________________________

Today I know you will you give me the strength to….

1. ______________________________

I praise you for all your mercies and blessings from today…

1. ______________________________
2. ______________________________
3. ______________________________

I lay the following prayers at your feet as I rest in your goodness…

1. ______________________________
2. ______________________________
3. ______________________________

Date ___ / ___ / ___

Lord, hear my prayer, listen to my cry for mercy;
in your faithfulness and righteousness come to my relief.

-Psalm 143:1

Father, I lift up the following in prayer as I start my day…

1. ______________________________
2. ______________________________
3. ______________________________

Father, I am thankful and grateful for….

1. ______________________________
2. ______________________________
3. ______________________________

Today I know you will you give me the strength to….

1. ______________________________

I praise you for all your mercies and blessings from today…

1. ______________________________
2. ______________________________
3. ______________________________

I lay the following prayers at your feet as I rest in your goodness…

1. ______________________________
2. ______________________________
3. ______________________________

Date ___ / ___ / ___

I have told you these things, so that in me you may have peace.
In this world you will have trouble.
But take heart! I have overcome the world.

-John 16:33

Father, I lift up the following in prayer as I start my day…

1. ______________________________
2. ______________________________
3. ______________________________

Father, I am thankful and grateful for….

1. ______________________________
2. ______________________________
3. ______________________________

Today I know you will you give me the strength to….

1. ______________________________

I praise you for all your mercies and blessings from today…

1. ______________________________
2. ______________________________
3. ______________________________

I lay the following prayers at your feet as I rest in your goodness…

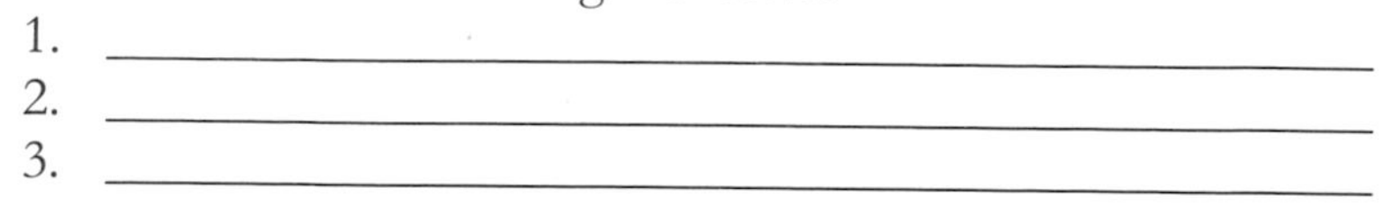

1. ______________________________
2. ______________________________
3. ______________________________

Date ___ / ___ / ___

Through these he has given us his very great and precious promises, so that through them you may participate in the divine nature, having escaped the corruption in the world caused by evil desires.

-2 Peter 1:4

Father, I lift up the following in prayer as I start my day…

1. ______________________________
2. ______________________________
3. ______________________________

Father, I am thankful and grateful for….

1. ______________________________
2. ______________________________
3. ______________________________

Today I know you will you give me the strength to….

1. ______________________________

I praise you for all your mercies and blessings from today…

1. ______________________________
2. ______________________________
3. ______________________________

I lay the following prayers at your feet as I rest in your goodness…

1. ______________________________
2. ______________________________
3. ______________________________

Date ___ / ___ / ___

I will glory in the Lord;
let the afflicted hear and rejoice.

-Psalm 34:2

Father, I lift up the following in prayer as I start my day…

1. ____________________
2. ____________________
3. ____________________

Father, I am thankful and grateful for….

1. ____________________
2. ____________________
3. ____________________

Today I know you will you give me the strength to….

1. ____________________

I praise you for all your mercies and blessings from today…

1. ____________________
2. ____________________
3. ____________________

I lay the following prayers at your feet as I rest in your goodness…

1. ____________________
2. ____________________
3. ____________________

Date ___ / ___ / ___

If we confess our sins, he is faithful and just and will forgive us our sins and purify us from all unrighteousness.

-1 John 1:9

Father, I lift up the following in prayer as I start my day…

1. ______________________________
2. ______________________________
3. ______________________________

Father, I am thankful and grateful for….

1. ______________________________
2. ______________________________
3. ______________________________

Today I know you will you give me the strength to….

1. ______________________________

I praise you for all your mercies and blessings from today…

1. ______________________________
2. ______________________________
3. ______________________________

I lay the following prayers at your feet as I rest in your goodness…

1. ______________________________
2. ______________________________
3. ______________________________

Date ___ / ___ / ___

But the fruit of the Spirit is love, joy, peace, patience, kindness, goodness, faithfulness, gentleness and self-control. Against such things there is no law.

-Galatians 5:22-23

Father, I lift up the following in prayer as I start my day…

1. ______________________________
2. ______________________________
3. ______________________________

Father, I am thankful and grateful for….

1. ______________________________
2. ______________________________
3. ______________________________

Today I know you will you give me the strength to….

1. ______________________________

I praise you for all your mercies and blessings from today…

1. ______________________________
2. ______________________________
3. ______________________________

I lay the following prayers at your feet as I rest in your goodness…

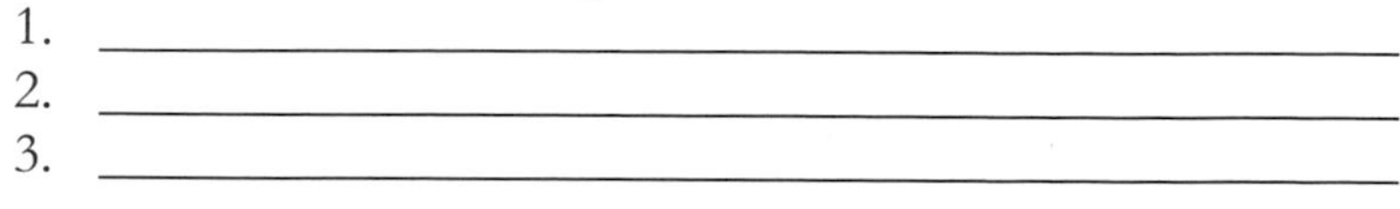

1. ______________________________
2. ______________________________
3. ______________________________

Date ___ / ___ / ___

Therefore, if anyone is in Christ, the new creation has come:
The old has gone, the new is here!

-2 Corinthians 5:17

Father, I lift up the following in prayer as I start my day…

1. ______________________________
2. ______________________________
3. ______________________________

Father, I am thankful and grateful for….

1. ______________________________
2. ______________________________
3. ______________________________

Today I know you will you give me the strength to….

1. ______________________________

I praise you for all your mercies and blessings from today…

1. ______________________________
2. ______________________________
3. ______________________________

I lay the following prayers at your feet as I rest in your goodness…

1. ______________________________
2. ______________________________
3. ______________________________

Date ___ / ___ / ___

The LORD will guide you always; he will satisfy your needs in a sun-scorched land and will strengthen your frame. You will be like a well-watered garden, like a spring whose waters never fail.

-Isaiah 58:11

Father, I lift up the following in prayer as I start my day…

1. ________________________________
2. ________________________________
3. ________________________________

Father, I am thankful and grateful for….

1. ________________________________
2. ________________________________
3. ________________________________

Today I know you will you give me the strength to….

1. ________________________________

I praise you for all your mercies and blessings from today…

1. ________________________________
2. ________________________________
3. ________________________________

I lay the following prayers at your feet as I rest in your goodness…

1. ________________________________
2. ________________________________
3. ________________________________

Date ___ / ___ / ___

Cast your cares on the Lord and he will sustain you;
he will never let the righteous be shaken.

-Psalm 55:22

Father, I lift up the following in prayer as I start my day…

1. ______________________________
2. ______________________________
3. ______________________________

Father, I am thankful and grateful for….

1. ______________________________
2. ______________________________
3. ______________________________

Today I know you will you give me the strength to….

1. ______________________________

I praise you for all your mercies and blessings from today…

1. ______________________________
2. ______________________________
3. ______________________________

I lay the following prayers at your feet as I rest in your goodness…

1. ______________________________
2. ______________________________
3. ______________________________

Date ___ / ___ / ___

For the wages of sin is death, but the gift of God
is eternal life in Christ Jesus our Lord.

-Romans 6:23

Father, I lift up the following in prayer as I start my day…

1. ____
2. ____
3. ____

Father, I am thankful and grateful for….

1. ____
2. ____
3. ____

Today I know you will you give me the strength to….

1. ____

I praise you for all your mercies and blessings from today…

1. ____
2. ____
3. ____

I lay the following prayers at your feet as I rest in your goodness…

1. ____
2. ____
3. ____

Date ___ / ___ / ___

The name of the LORD is a fortified tower;
the righteous run to it and are safe.

-Proverbs 18:10

Father, I lift up the following in prayer as I start my day…

1. ______________________________
2. ______________________________
3. ______________________________

Father, I am thankful and grateful for….

1. ______________________________
2. ______________________________
3. ______________________________

Today I know you will you give me the strength to….

1. ______________________________

I praise you for all your mercies and blessings from today…

1. ______________________________
2. ______________________________
3. ______________________________

I lay the following prayers at your feet as I rest in your goodness…

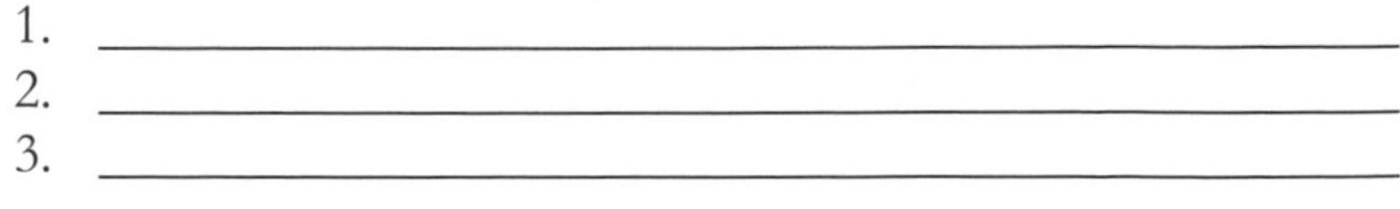

Date ___ / ___ / ___

And lead us not into temptation,
but deliver us from the evil one.

-Matthew 6:13

Father, I lift up the following in prayer as I start my day…

1. ______________________________
2. ______________________________
3. ______________________________

Father, I am thankful and grateful for….

1. ______________________________
2. ______________________________
3. ______________________________

Today I know you will you give me the strength to….

1. ______________________________

I praise you for all your mercies and blessings from today…

1. ______________________________
2. ______________________________
3. ______________________________

I lay the following prayers at your feet as I rest in your goodness…

1. ______________________________
2. ______________________________
3. ______________________________

Date ___ / ___ / ___

And if we know that he hears us—whatever we ask—
we know that we have what we asked of him.

-1 John 5:15

Father, I lift up the following in prayer as I start my day…

1. ______________________________
2. ______________________________
3. ______________________________

Father, I am thankful and grateful for….

1. ______________________________
2. ______________________________
3. ______________________________

Today I know you will you give me the strength to….

1. ______________________________

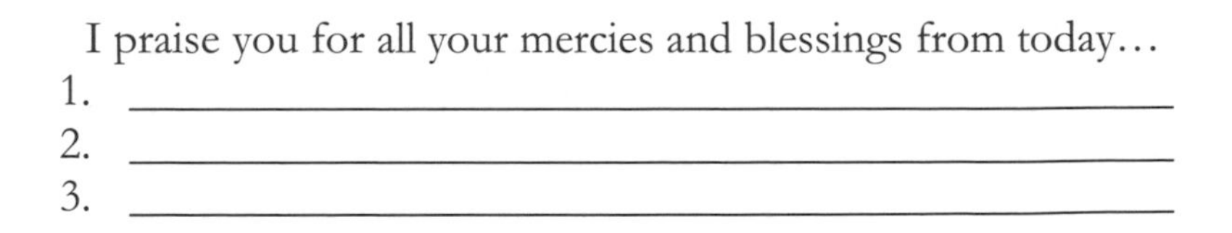

I praise you for all your mercies and blessings from today…

1. ______________________________
2. ______________________________
3. ______________________________

I lay the following prayers at your feet as I rest in your goodness…

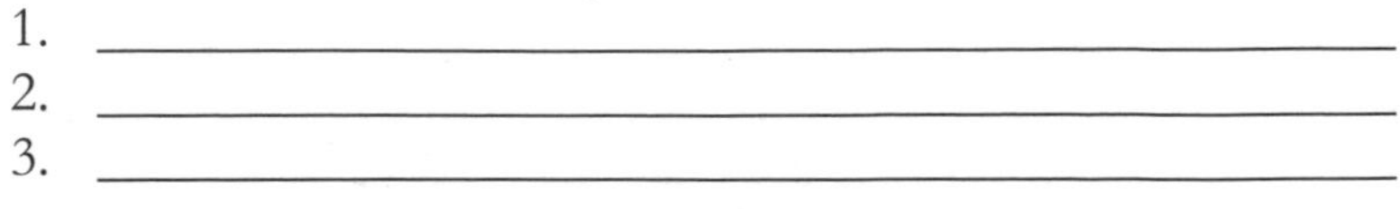

1. ______________________________
2. ______________________________
3. ______________________________

Date ___ / ___ / ___

Consider it pure joy…whenever you face trials of many kinds, because you know that the testing of your faith produces perseverance. Let perseverance finish its work so that you may be mature and complete, not lacking anything.

-James 1:2-4

Father, I lift up the following in prayer as I start my day…

1. ______________________________
2. ______________________________
3. ______________________________

Father, I am thankful and grateful for….

1. ______________________________
2. ______________________________
3. ______________________________

Today I know you will you give me the strength to….

1. ______________________________

I praise you for all your mercies and blessings from today…

1. ______________________________
2. ______________________________
3. ______________________________

I lay the following prayers at your feet as I rest in your goodness…

1. ______________________________
2. ______________________________
3. ______________________________

Date ___ / ___ / ___

Finally, brothers, whatever is true, whatever is noble, whatever is right, whatever is pure, whatever is lovely, whatever is admirable—if anything is excellent or praiseworthy—think about such things.

-Philippians 4:8

Father, I lift up the following in prayer as I start my day…

1. ______________________________
2. ______________________________
3. ______________________________

Father, I am thankful and grateful for….

1. ______________________________
2. ______________________________
3. ______________________________

Today I know you will you give me the strength to….

1. ______________________________

I praise you for all your mercies and blessings from today…

1. ______________________________
2. ______________________________
3. ______________________________

I lay the following prayers at your feet as I rest in your goodness…

1. ______________________________
2. ______________________________
3. ______________________________

Date ___ / ___ / ___

Open my lips, Lord, and my
mouth will declare your praise.

-Psalm 51:15

Father, I lift up the following in prayer as I start my day…

1. ______________________________
2. ______________________________
3. ______________________________

Father, I am thankful and grateful for….

1. ______________________________
2. ______________________________
3. ______________________________

Today I know you will you give me the strength to….

1. ______________________________

I praise you for all your mercies and blessings from today…

1. ______________________________
2. ______________________________
3. ______________________________

I lay the following prayers at your feet as I rest in your goodness…

1. ______________________________
2. ______________________________
3. ______________________________

Date ___ / ___ / ___

Therefore do not worry about tomorrow, for tomorrow will worry about itself. Each day has enough troubles of its own.

-Matthew 6:34

Father, I lift up the following in prayer as I start my day…

1. ______________________________
2. ______________________________
3. ______________________________

Father, I am thankful and grateful for….

1. ______________________________
2. ______________________________
3. ______________________________

Today I know you will you give me the strength to….

1. ______________________________

I praise you for all your mercies and blessings from today…

1. ______________________________
2. ______________________________
3. ______________________________

I lay the following prayers at your feet as I rest in your goodness…

1. ______________________________
2. ______________________________
3. ______________________________

Date ___ / ___ / ___

…no weapon forged against you will prevail, and you will refute every tongue that accuses you. This is the heritage of the servants of the Lord, and this is their vindication from me," declares the Lord.

-Isaiah 54:17

Father, I lift up the following in prayer as I start my day…

1. ______________________________
2. ______________________________
3. ______________________________

Father, I am thankful and grateful for….

1. ______________________________
2. ______________________________
3. ______________________________

Today I know you will you give me the strength to….

1. ______________________________

I praise you for all your mercies and blessings from today…

1. ______________________________
2. ______________________________
3. ______________________________

I lay the following prayers at your feet as I rest in your goodness…

1. ______________________________
2. ______________________________
3. ______________________________

Date ___ / ___ / ___

I cried out to him with my mouth;
his praise was on my tongue.

-Psalm 66:17

Father, I lift up the following in prayer as I start my day…

1. ______________________________
2. ______________________________
3. ______________________________

Father, I am thankful and grateful for….

1. ______________________________
2. ______________________________
3. ______________________________

Today I know you will you give me the strength to….

1. ______________________________

I praise you for all your mercies and blessings from today…

1. ______________________________
2. ______________________________
3. ______________________________

I lay the following prayers at your feet as I rest in your goodness…

1. ______________________________
2. ______________________________
3. ______________________________

Date ___ / ___ / ___

So we fasted and petitioned our God about this,
and he answered our prayer.

-Ezra 8:23

Father, I lift up the following in prayer as I start my day…

1. ______________________________
2. ______________________________
3. ______________________________

Father, I am thankful and grateful for….

1. ______________________________
2. ______________________________
3. ______________________________

Today I know you will you give me the strength to….

1. ______________________________

I praise you for all your mercies and blessings from today…

1. ______________________________
2. ______________________________
3. ______________________________

I lay the following prayers at your feet as I rest in your goodness…

1. ______________________________
2. ______________________________
3. ______________________________

Date ___ / ___ / ___

By day the Lord directs his love, at night his song is with me—
a prayer to the God of my life.

-Psalm 42:8

Father, I lift up the following in prayer as I start my day…

1. ______________________________
2. ______________________________
3. ______________________________

Father, I am thankful and grateful for….

1. ______________________________
2. ______________________________
3. ______________________________

Today I know you will you give me the strength to….

1. ______________________________

I praise you for all your mercies and blessings from today…

1. ______________________________
2. ______________________________
3. ______________________________

I lay the following prayers at your feet as I rest in your goodness…

1. ______________________________
2. ______________________________
3. ______________________________

Date ___ / ___ / ___

I lift up my eyes to the mountains—where does my help come from? My help comes from the Lord, the Maker of heaven and earth.

-Psalm 121:1-2

Father, I lift up the following in prayer as I start my day…

1. ____
2. ____
3. ____

Father, I am thankful and grateful for….

1. ____
2. ____
3. ____

Today I know you will you give me the strength to….

1. ____

I praise you for all your mercies and blessings from today…

1. ____
2. ____
3. ____

I lay the following prayers at your feet as I rest in your goodness…

1. ____
2. ____
3. ____

Date ___ / ___ / ___

Yet to all who received him, to those who believed in his name, he gave the right to become children of God

-John 1:12

Father, I lift up the following in prayer as I start my day…

1. ____________________
2. ____________________
3. ____________________

Father, I am thankful and grateful for….

1. ____________________
2. ____________________
3. ____________________

Today I know you will you give me the strength to….

1. ____________________

I praise you for all your mercies and blessings from today…

1. ____________________
2. ____________________
3. ____________________

I lay the following prayers at your feet as I rest in your goodness…

1. ____________________
2. ____________________
3. ____________________

Date ___ / ___ / ___

May the favor of the Lord our God rest on us; establish the work of our hands for us—yes, establish the work of our hands.

-Psalm 90:17

Father, I lift up the following in prayer as I start my day…

1. ______________________________
2. ______________________________
3. ______________________________

Father, I am thankful and grateful for….

1. ______________________________
2. ______________________________
3. ______________________________

Today I know you will you give me the strength to….

1. ______________________________

I praise you for all your mercies and blessings from today…

1. ______________________________
2. ______________________________
3. ______________________________

I lay the following prayers at your feet as I rest in your goodness…

1. ______________________________
2. ______________________________
3. ______________________________

Date ___ / ___ / ___

This is the confidence we have before Him, that, if we ask anything according to His will, He hears us. And if we know that He hears us in whatever we ask, we know that we have the requests which we have asked from Him.

-John 5:14-15

Father, I lift up the following in prayer as I start my day…

1. ______________________________
2. ______________________________
3. ______________________________

Father, I am thankful and grateful for….

1. ______________________________
2. ______________________________
3. ______________________________

Today I know you will you give me the strength to….

1. ______________________________

I praise you for all your mercies and blessings from today…

1. ______________________________
2. ______________________________
3. ______________________________

I lay the following prayers at your feet as I rest in your goodness…

1. ______________________________
2. ______________________________
3. ______________________________

Date ___ / ___ / ___

…but those who hope in the LORD will renew their strength.
They will soar on wings like eagles; they will run and not grow weary,
they will walk and not be faint.

-Isaiah 40:31

Father, I lift up the following in prayer as I start my day…

1. ______________________________
2. ______________________________
3. ______________________________

Father, I am thankful and grateful for….

1. ______________________________
2. ______________________________
3. ______________________________

Today I know you will you give me the strength to….

1. ______________________________

I praise you for all your mercies and blessings from today…

1. ______________________________
2. ______________________________
3. ______________________________

I lay the following prayers at your feet as I rest in your goodness…

1. ______________________________
2. ______________________________
3. ______________________________

Date ___ / ___ / ___

For I know that through your prayers and God's provision of the Spirit of Jesus Christ what has happened to me will turn out for my deliverance.

-Philippians 1:19

Father, I lift up the following in prayer as I start my day…

1. ______________________________
2. ______________________________
3. ______________________________

Father, I am thankful and grateful for….

1. ______________________________
2. ______________________________
3. ______________________________

Today I know you will you give me the strength to….

1. ______________________________

I praise you for all your mercies and blessings from today…

1. ______________________________
2. ______________________________
3. ______________________________

I lay the following prayers at your feet as I rest in your goodness…

1. ______________________________
2. ______________________________
3. ______________________________

Date ___ / ___ / ___

Very truly I tell you, whoever hears my word and believes him who sent me has eternal life and will not be judged but has crossed over from death to life.

-John 5:24

Father, I lift up the following in prayer as I start my day…

1. ______________________________
2. ______________________________
3. ______________________________

Father, I am thankful and grateful for….

1. ______________________________
2. ______________________________
3. ______________________________

Today I know you will you give me the strength to….

1. ______________________________

I praise you for all your mercies and blessings from today…

1. ______________________________
2. ______________________________
3. ______________________________

I lay the following prayers at your feet as I rest in your goodness…

1. ______________________________
2. ______________________________
3. ______________________________

Date ___ / ___ / ___

If you believe, you will receive
whatever you ask for in prayer.

-Matthew 21:22

Father, I lift up the following in prayer as I start my day…

1. ______________________________
2. ______________________________
3. ______________________________

Father, I am thankful and grateful for….

1. ______________________________
2. ______________________________
3. ______________________________

Today I know you will you give me the strength to….

1. ______________________________

I praise you for all your mercies and blessings from today…

1. ______________________________
2. ______________________________
3. ______________________________

I lay the following prayers at your feet as I rest in your goodness…

1. ______________________________
2. ______________________________
3. ______________________________

Date ___ / ___ / ___

And the peace of God, which transcends all understanding, will guard your hearts and your minds in Christ Jesus.

-Philippians 4:7

Father, I lift up the following in prayer as I start my day…

1. ______________________________
2. ______________________________
3. ______________________________

Father, I am thankful and grateful for….

1. ______________________________
2. ______________________________
3. ______________________________

Today I know you will you give me the strength to….

1. ______________________________

I praise you for all your mercies and blessings from today…

1. ______________________________
2. ______________________________
3. ______________________________

I lay the following prayers at your feet as I rest in your goodness…

1. ______________________________
2. ______________________________
3. ______________________________

Date ___ / ___ / ___

I call on the Lord in my distress,
and he answers me.

-Psalm 120:1

Father, I lift up the following in prayer as I start my day…

1. ______________________________
2. ______________________________
3. ______________________________

Father, I am thankful and grateful for….

1. ______________________________
2. ______________________________
3. ______________________________

Today I know you will you give me the strength to….

1. ______________________________

I praise you for all your mercies and blessings from today…

1. ______________________________
2. ______________________________
3. ______________________________

I lay the following prayers at your feet as I rest in your goodness…

1. ______________________________
2. ______________________________
3. ______________________________

Date ___ / ___ / ___

Consequently, faith comes from hearing the message,
and the message is heard through the word of Christ.

-Romans 5:17

Father, I lift up the following in prayer as I start my day…

1. ______________________________
2. ______________________________
3. ______________________________

Father, I am thankful and grateful for….

1. ______________________________
2. ______________________________
3. ______________________________

Today I know you will you give me the strength to….

1. ______________________________

I praise you for all your mercies and blessings from today…

1. ______________________________
2. ______________________________
3. ______________________________

I lay the following prayers at your feet as I rest in your goodness…

1. ______________________________
2. ______________________________
3. ______________________________

Date ___ / ___ / ___

The Lord will keep you from all harm—he will watch over your life; the Lord will watch over your coming and going both now and forevermore.

-Psalm 121:7-8

Father, I lift up the following in prayer as I start my day…

1. ________________________________
2. ________________________________
3. ________________________________

Father, I am thankful and grateful for….

1. ________________________________
2. ________________________________
3. ________________________________

Today I know you will you give me the strength to….

1. ________________________________

I praise you for all your mercies and blessings from today…

1. ________________________________
2. ________________________________
3. ________________________________

I lay the following prayers at your feet as I rest in your goodness…

1. ________________________________
2. ________________________________
3. ________________________________

Date ___ / ___ / ___

I will give you a new heart and put a new spirit within you;
I will remove your heart of stone and give you a heart of flesh.

-Ezekiel 36:26

Father, I lift up the following in prayer as I start my day…

1. ______________________________
2. ______________________________
3. ______________________________

Father, I am thankful and grateful for….

1. ______________________________
2. ______________________________
3. ______________________________

Today I know you will you give me the strength to….

1. ______________________________

I praise you for all your mercies and blessings from today…

1. ______________________________
2. ______________________________
3. ______________________________

I lay the following prayers at your feet as I rest in your goodness…

1. ______________________________
2. ______________________________
3. ______________________________

Date ___ / ___ / ___

So do not fear, for I am with you; do not be dismayed,
for I am your God. I will strengthen you and help you;
I will uphold you with my righteous right hand.

-Isaiah 41:10

Father, I lift up the following in prayer as I start my day…

1. ____
2. ____
3. ____

Father, I am thankful and grateful for….

1. ____
2. ____
3. ____

Today I know you will you give me the strength to….

1. ____

I praise you for all your mercies and blessings from today…

1. ____
2. ____
3. ____

I lay the following prayers at your feet as I rest in your goodness…

1. ____
2. ____
3. ____

Date ___ / ___ / ___

Peace I leave with you; my peace I give you.
I do not give to you as the world gives.
Do not let your hearts be troubled and do not be afraid.

-John 14:27

Father, I lift up the following in prayer as I start my day…

1. ____________________
2. ____________________
3. ____________________

Father, I am thankful and grateful for….

1. ____________________
2. ____________________
3. ____________________

Today I know you will you give me the strength to….

1. ____________________

I praise you for all your mercies and blessings from today…

1. ____________________
2. ____________________
3. ____________________

I lay the following prayers at your feet as I rest in your goodness…

1. ____________________
2. ____________________
3. ____________________

Date ___ / ___ / ___

Do not conform to the pattern of this world, but be transformed by the renewing of your mind. Then you will be able to test and approve what God's will is—his good, pleasing and perfect will.

-Romans 12:2

Father, I lift up the following in prayer as I start my day…

1. ________________________________
2. ________________________________
3. ________________________________

Father, I am thankful and grateful for….

1. ________________________________
2. ________________________________
3. ________________________________

Today I know you will you give me the strength to….

1. ________________________________

I praise you for all your mercies and blessings from today…

1. ________________________________
2. ________________________________
3. ________________________________

I lay the following prayers at your feet as I rest in your goodness…

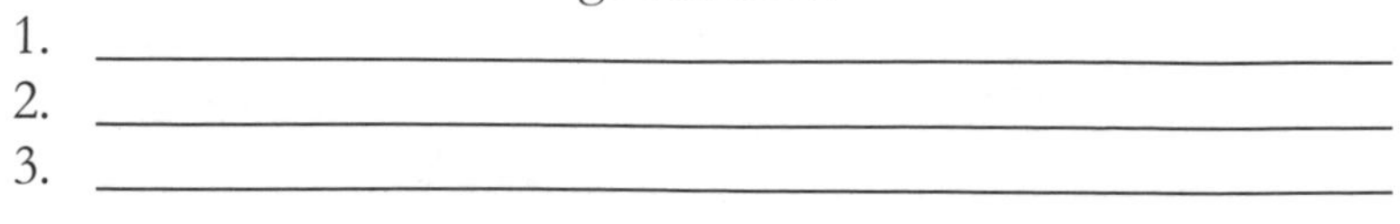

1. ________________________________
2. ________________________________
3. ________________________________

Date ___ / ___ / ___

Go and make disciples of all nations, baptizing them in the name of the Father and of the Son and of the Holy Spirit. and teaching them to obey everything I have commanded you. And surely I am with you always, to the end of the age.

Matthew 28:19-20

Father, I lift up the following in prayer as I start my day…

1. ________________________________
2. ________________________________
3. ________________________________

Father, I am thankful and grateful for….

1. ________________________________
2. ________________________________
3. ________________________________

Today I know you will you give me the strength to….

1. ________________________________

I praise you for all your mercies and blessings from today…

1. ________________________________
2. ________________________________
3. ________________________________

I lay the following prayers at your feet as I rest in your goodness…

1. ________________________________
2. ________________________________
3. ________________________________

Date ___ / ___ / ___

Take my yoke upon you and learn from me, for I am gentle and humble in heart, and you will find rest for your souls. For my yoke is easy and my burden is light

-Matthew 11:29-30

Father, I lift up the following in prayer as I start my day…

1. ______________________________
2. ______________________________
3. ______________________________

Father, I am thankful and grateful for….

1. ______________________________
2. ______________________________
3. ______________________________

Today I know you will you give me the strength to….

1. ______________________________

I praise you for all your mercies and blessings from today…

1. ______________________________
2. ______________________________
3. ______________________________

I lay the following prayers at your feet as I rest in your goodness…

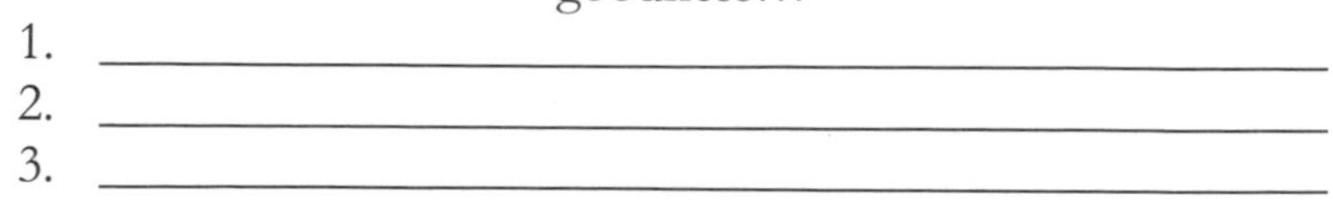

1. ______________________________
2. ______________________________
3. ______________________________

Date ___ / ___ / ___

The Lord is near to all who call on him,
to all who call on him in truth.

-Psalm 145:18

Father, I lift up the following in prayer as I start my day…

1. ______________________________
2. ______________________________
3. ______________________________

Father, I am thankful and grateful for….

1. ______________________________
2. ______________________________
3. ______________________________

Today I know you will you give me the strength to….

1. ______________________________

I praise you for all your mercies and blessings from today…

1. ______________________________
2. ______________________________
3. ______________________________

I lay the following prayers at your feet as I rest in your goodness…

1. ______________________________
2. ______________________________
3. ______________________________

Date ___ / ___ / ___

After they prayed, the place where they were meeting was shaken. And they were all filled with the Holy Spirit and spoke the word of God boldly.

-Acts 4:31

Father, I lift up the following in prayer as I start my day…

1. ______________________________
2. ______________________________
3. ______________________________

Father, I am thankful and grateful for….

1. ______________________________
2. ______________________________
3. ______________________________

Today I know you will you give me the strength to….

1. ______________________________

I praise you for all your mercies and blessings from today…

1. ______________________________
2. ______________________________
3. ______________________________

I lay the following prayers at your feet as I rest in your goodness…

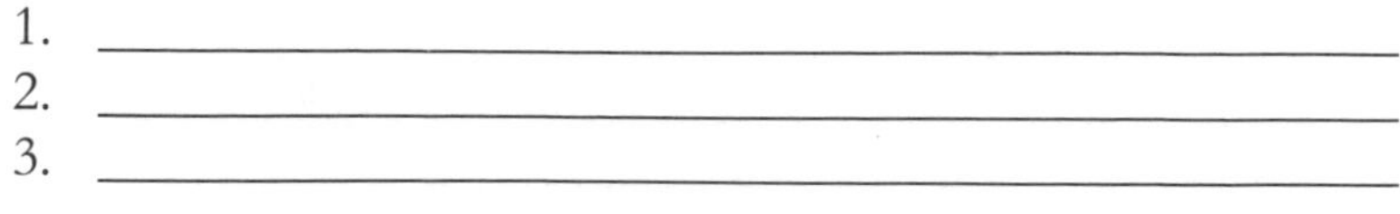

1. ______________________________
2. ______________________________
3. ______________________________

Date ___ / ___ / ___

Very truly I tell you,
the one who believes has eternal life.

-John 6:47

Father, I lift up the following in prayer as I start my day…

1. ____________________
2. ____________________
3. ____________________

Father, I am thankful and grateful for….

1. ____________________
2. ____________________
3. ____________________

Today I know you will you give me the strength to….

1. ____________________

I praise you for all your mercies and blessings from today…

1. ____________________
2. ____________________
3. ____________________

I lay the following prayers at your feet as I rest in your goodness…

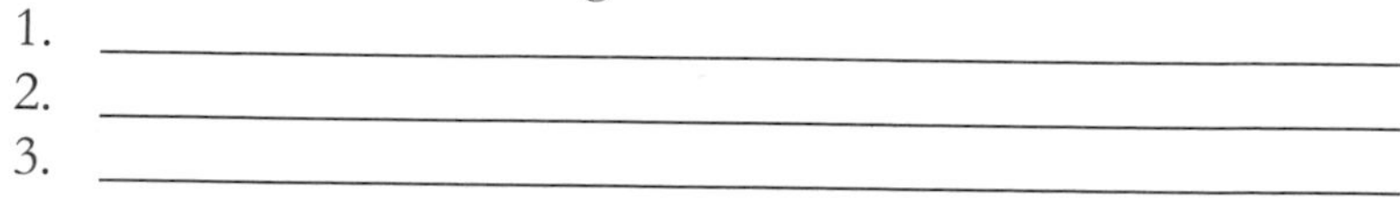

1. ____________________
2. ____________________
3. ____________________

Date ___ / ___ / ___

The mind governed by the flesh is death,
but the mind governed by the Spirit is life and peace.

-Romans 8:6

Father, I lift up the following in prayer as I start my day…

1. ______________________________
2. ______________________________
3. ______________________________

Father, I am thankful and grateful for….

1. ______________________________
2. ______________________________
3. ______________________________

Today I know you will you give me the strength to….

1. ______________________________

I praise you for all your mercies and blessings from today…

1. ______________________________
2. ______________________________
3. ______________________________

I lay the following prayers at your feet as I rest in your goodness…

1. ______________________________
2. ______________________________
3. ______________________________

Date ___ / ___ / ___

The Lord your God is with you, the Mighty Warrior who saves.
He will take great delight in you; in his love he will no longer rebuke you
but will rejoice over you with singing."

-Zephaniah 3:17

Father, I lift up the following in prayer as I start my day…

1. ________________________________
2. ________________________________
3. ________________________________

Father, I am thankful and grateful for….

1. ________________________________
2. ________________________________
3. ________________________________

Today I know you will you give me the strength to….

1. ________________________________

I praise you for all your mercies and blessings from today…

1. ________________________________
2. ________________________________
3. ________________________________

I lay the following prayers at your feet as I rest in your goodness…

1. ________________________________
2. ________________________________
3. ________________________________

Date ___ / ___ / ___

All Scripture is God-breathed and is useful for teaching, rebuking, correcting and training in righteousness, so that the servant of God may be thoroughly equipped for every good work.

-2 Timothy 3:16-17

Father, I lift up the following in prayer as I start my day…

1. ______________________________
2. ______________________________
3. ______________________________

Father, I am thankful and grateful for….

1. ______________________________
2. ______________________________
3. ______________________________

Today I know you will you give me the strength to….

1. ______________________________

I praise you for all your mercies and blessings from today…

1. ______________________________
2. ______________________________
3. ______________________________

I lay the following prayers at your feet as I rest in your goodness…

1. ______________________________
2. ______________________________
3. ______________________________

Date ___ / ___ / ___

In the same way, the Spirit helps us in our weakness.
We do not know what we ought to pray for,
but the Spirit himself intercedes for us through wordless groans.

-Romans 8:26

Father, I lift up the following in prayer as I start my day…

1. ______________________________
2. ______________________________
3. ______________________________

Father, I am thankful and grateful for….

1. ______________________________
2. ______________________________
3. ______________________________

Today I know you will you give me the strength to….

1. ______________________________

I praise you for all your mercies and blessings from today…

1. ______________________________
2. ______________________________
3. ______________________________

I lay the following prayers at your feet as I rest in your goodness…

1. ______________________________
2. ______________________________
3. ______________________________

Date ___ / ___ / ___

…we are afflicted in every way, but not crushed; perplexed, but not despairing; persecuted, but not forsaken; struck down, but not destroyed;

-2 Corinthians 4:8-9

Father, I lift up the following in prayer as I start my day…

1. ______________________________
2. ______________________________
3. ______________________________

Father, I am thankful and grateful for….

1. ______________________________
2. ______________________________
3. ______________________________

Today I know you will you give me the strength to….

1. ______________________________

I praise you for all your mercies and blessings from today…

1. ______________________________
2. ______________________________
3. ______________________________

I lay the following prayers at your feet as I rest in your goodness…

1. ______________________________
2. ______________________________
3. ______________________________

Date ___ / ___ / ___

Be joyful in hope, patient in affliction,
faithful in prayer.

-Romans 12:12

Father, I lift up the following in prayer as I start my day…

1. ______________________________
2. ______________________________
3. ______________________________

Father, I am thankful and grateful for….

1. ______________________________
2. ______________________________
3. ______________________________

Today I know you will you give me the strength to….

1. ______________________________

I praise you for all your mercies and blessings from today…

1. ______________________________
2. ______________________________
3. ______________________________

I lay the following prayers at your feet as I rest in your goodness…

1. ______________________________
2. ______________________________
3. ______________________________

Date ___ / ___ / ___

You did not choose me, but I chose you and appointed you so that you might go and bear fruit—fruit that will last—and so that whatever you ask in my name the Father will give you.

-John 15:16

Father, I lift up the following in prayer as I start my day…

1. ______________________________
2. ______________________________
3. ______________________________

Father, I am thankful and grateful for….

1. ______________________________
2. ______________________________
3. ______________________________

Today I know you will you give me the strength to….

1. ______________________________

I praise you for all your mercies and blessings from today…

1. ______________________________
2. ______________________________
3. ______________________________

I lay the following prayers at your feet as I rest in your goodness…

1. ______________________________
2. ______________________________
3. ______________________________

Date ___ / ___ / ___

And I will do whatever you ask in my name,
so that the Father may be glorified in the Son.

-John 14:13

Father, I lift up the following in prayer as I start my day…

1. ______________________________
2. ______________________________
3. ______________________________

Father, I am thankful and grateful for….

1. ______________________________
2. ______________________________
3. ______________________________

Today I know you will you give me the strength to….

1. ______________________________

I praise you for all your mercies and blessings from today…

1. ______________________________
2. ______________________________
3. ______________________________

I lay the following prayers at your feet as I rest in your goodness…

1. ______________________________
2. ______________________________
3. ______________________________

Date ___ / ___ / ___

But to you who are listening I say: Love your enemies, do good to those who hate you, bless those who curse you, pray for those who mistreat you.

-Luke 6:27-28

Father, I lift up the following in prayer as I start my day…

1. ______________________________
2. ______________________________
3. ______________________________

Father, I am thankful and grateful for….

1. ______________________________
2. ______________________________
3. ______________________________

Today I know you will you give me the strength to….

1. ______________________________

I praise you for all your mercies and blessings from today…

1. ______________________________
2. ______________________________
3. ______________________________

I lay the following prayers at your feet as I rest in your goodness…

1. ______________________________
2. ______________________________
3. ______________________________

Date ___ / ___ / ___

Take delight in the Lord, and he will give you the desires of your heart.

-Psalm 37:4

Father, I lift up the following in prayer as I start my day…

1. ______________________________
2. ______________________________
3. ______________________________

Father, I am thankful and grateful for….

1. ______________________________
2. ______________________________
3. ______________________________

Today I know you will you give me the strength to….

1. ______________________________

I praise you for all your mercies and blessings from today…

1. ______________________________
2. ______________________________
3. ______________________________

I lay the following prayers at your feet as I rest in your goodness…

1. ______________________________
2. ______________________________
3. ______________________________

Date ___ / ___ / ___

Blessed is the one who perseveres under trial because, having stood the test, that person will receive the crown of life that the Lord has promised to those who love him.

-James 1:12

Father, I lift up the following in prayer as I start my day…

1. ______________________________
2. ______________________________
3. ______________________________

Father, I am thankful and grateful for….

1. ______________________________
2. ______________________________
3. ______________________________

Today I know you will you give me the strength to….

1. ______________________________

I praise you for all your mercies and blessings from today…

1. ______________________________
2. ______________________________
3. ______________________________

I lay the following prayers at your feet as I rest in your goodness…

1. ______________________________
2. ______________________________
3. ______________________________

Date ___ / ___ / ___

But you will receive power when the Holy Spirit comes on you; and you will be my witnesses in Jerusalem, and in all Judea and Samaria, and to the ends of the earth.

-Acts 1:8

Father, I lift up the following in prayer as I start my day…

1. ______________________________
2. ______________________________
3. ______________________________

Father, I am thankful and grateful for….

1. ______________________________
2. ______________________________
3. ______________________________

Today I know you will you give me the strength to….

1. ______________________________

I praise you for all your mercies and blessings from today…

1. ______________________________
2. ______________________________
3. ______________________________

I lay the following prayers at your feet as I rest in your goodness…

1. ______________________________
2. ______________________________
3. ______________________________

Date ___ / ___ / ___

One thing I ask from the Lord, this only do I seek:
that I may dwell in the house of the Lord all the days of my life,
to gaze on the beauty of the Lord and to seek him in his temple.

-Psalm 27:4

Father, I lift up the following in prayer as I start my day…

1. ______________________________
2. ______________________________
3. ______________________________

Father, I am thankful and grateful for….

1. ______________________________
2. ______________________________
3. ______________________________

Today I know you will you give me the strength to….

1. ______________________________

I praise you for all your mercies and blessings from today…

1. ______________________________
2. ______________________________
3. ______________________________

I lay the following prayers at your feet as I rest in your goodness…

1. ______________________________
2. ______________________________
3. ______________________________

Date ___ / ___ / ___

Even though I walk through the darkest valley,
I will fear no evil, for you are with me;
your rod and your staff, they comfort me.

-Psalm 23:4

Father, I lift up the following in prayer as I start my day…

1. ______________________________
2. ______________________________
3. ______________________________

Father, I am thankful and grateful for….

1. ______________________________
2. ______________________________
3. ______________________________

Today I know you will you give me the strength to….

1. ______________________________

I praise you for all your mercies and blessings from today…

1. ______________________________
2. ______________________________
3. ______________________________

I lay the following prayers at your feet as I rest in your goodness…

1. ______________________________
2. ______________________________
3. ______________________________

Date ___ / ___ / ___

The One who calls you is faithful,
and He will do it.

-1 Thessalonians 5:24

Father, I lift up the following in prayer as I start my day…

1. ______________________________
2. ______________________________
3. ______________________________

Father, I am thankful and grateful for….

1. ______________________________
2. ______________________________
3. ______________________________

Today I know you will you give me the strength to….

1. ______________________________

I praise you for all your mercies and blessings from today…

1. ______________________________
2. ______________________________
3. ______________________________

I lay the following prayers at your feet as I rest in your goodness…

1. ______________________________
2. ______________________________
3. ______________________________

Date ___ / ___ / ___

Dear friend, I pray that you may enjoy good health and that all may go well with you, even as your soul is getting along well.

-3 John 1:2

Father, I lift up the following in prayer as I start my day…

1. ______________________________
2. ______________________________
3. ______________________________

Father, I am thankful and grateful for….

1. ______________________________
2. ______________________________
3. ______________________________

Today I know you will you give me the strength to….

1. ______________________________

I praise you for all your mercies and blessings from today…

1. ______________________________
2. ______________________________
3. ______________________________

I lay the following prayers at your feet as I rest in your goodness…

1. ______________________________
2. ______________________________
3. ______________________________

Reminder:

You only have two weeks of journal pages left!

We recommend that you order your next
Four-Minute Prayer Journal from our website so you can
continue your outstanding habit of prayer journaling!

FourMinutePrayerJournal.com

Date ___ / ___ / ___

But in your hearts set apart Christ as Lord. Always be prepared to give an answer to everyone who asks you to give the reason for the hope that you have. But do this with gentleness and respect,

-1 Peter 3:15

Father, I lift up the following in prayer as I start my day…

1. ______________________________
2. ______________________________
3. ______________________________

Father, I am thankful and grateful for….

1. ______________________________
2. ______________________________
3. ______________________________

Today I know you will you give me the strength to….

1. ______________________________

I praise you for all your mercies and blessings from today…

1. ______________________________
2. ______________________________
3. ______________________________

I lay the following prayers at your feet as I rest in your goodness…

1. ______________________________
2. ______________________________
3. ______________________________

Date ___ / ___ / ___

But now, this is what the LORD says— he who created you, O Jacob, he who formed you, O Israel: "Fear not, for I have redeemed you; I have summoned you by name; you are mine.

-Isaiah 43:1

Father, I lift up the following in prayer as I start my day…

1. ______________________
2. ______________________
3. ______________________

Father, I am thankful and grateful for….

1. ______________________
2. ______________________
3. ______________________

Today I know you will you give me the strength to….

1. ______________________

I praise you for all your mercies and blessings from today…

1. ______________________
2. ______________________
3. ______________________

I lay the following prayers at your feet as I rest in your goodness…

1. ______________________
2. ______________________
3. ______________________

Date ___ / ___ / ___

For in this hope we were saved;
but hope that is seen is no hope at all.
Who hopes for what he can already see?

-Romans 8:24

Father, I lift up the following in prayer as I start my day…

1. ______________________________
2. ______________________________
3. ______________________________

Father, I am thankful and grateful for….

1. ______________________________
2. ______________________________
3. ______________________________

Today I know you will you give me the strength to….

1. ______________________________

I praise you for all your mercies and blessings from today…

1. ______________________________
2. ______________________________
3. ______________________________

I lay the following prayers at your feet as I rest in your goodness…

1. ______________________________
2. ______________________________
3. ______________________________

Date ___ / ___ / ___

You, dear children, are from God and have overcome them, because the one who is in you is greater than the one who is in the world

-1 John 4:4

Father, I lift up the following in prayer as I start my day…

1. ______________________________
2. ______________________________
3. ______________________________

Father, I am thankful and grateful for….

1. ______________________________
2. ______________________________
3. ______________________________

Today I know you will you give me the strength to….

1. ______________________________

I praise you for all your mercies and blessings from today…

1. ______________________________
2. ______________________________
3. ______________________________

I lay the following prayers at your feet as I rest in your goodness…

1. ______________________________
2. ______________________________
3. ______________________________

Date ___ / ___ / ___

After Job had prayed for his friends, the Lord restored his fortunes and gave him twice as much as he had before.

-Job 42:10

Father, I lift up the following in prayer as I start my day…

1. ______________________________
2. ______________________________
3. ______________________________

Father, I am thankful and grateful for….

1. ______________________________
2. ______________________________
3. ______________________________

Today I know you will you give me the strength to….

1. ______________________________

I praise you for all your mercies and blessings from today…

1. ______________________________
2. ______________________________
3. ______________________________

I lay the following prayers at your feet as I rest in your goodness…

1. ______________________________
2. ______________________________
3. ______________________________

Date ___ / ___ / ___

There is no fear in love. But perfect love drives out fear, because fear has to do with punishment. The one who fears is not made perfect in love.

-1 John 4:18

Father, I lift up the following in prayer as I start my day…

1. ______________________________
2. ______________________________
3. ______________________________

Father, I am thankful and grateful for….

1. ______________________________
2. ______________________________
3. ______________________________

Today I know you will you give me the strength to….

1. ______________________________

I praise you for all your mercies and blessings from today…

1. ______________________________
2. ______________________________
3. ______________________________

I lay the following prayers at your feet as I rest in your goodness…

1. ______________________________
2. ______________________________
3. ______________________________

Date ___ / ___ / ___

He holds success in store for the upright,
he is a shield to those whose walk is blameless,

-Proverbs 2:7

Father, I lift up the following in prayer as I start my day…

1. ______________________________
2. ______________________________
3. ______________________________

Father, I am thankful and grateful for….

1. ______________________________
2. ______________________________
3. ______________________________

Today I know you will you give me the strength to….

1. ______________________________

I praise you for all your mercies and blessings from today…

1. ______________________________
2. ______________________________
3. ______________________________

I lay the following prayers at your feet as I rest in your goodness…

1. ______________________________
2. ______________________________
3. ______________________________

Date ___ / ___ / ___

For all have sinned and
fall short of the glory of God,

-Romans 3:23

Father, I lift up the following in prayer as I start my day…

1. ______________________________
2. ______________________________
3. ______________________________

Father, I am thankful and grateful for….

1. ______________________________
2. ______________________________
3. ______________________________

Today I know you will you give me the strength to….

1. ______________________________

I praise you for all your mercies and blessings from today…

1. ______________________________
2. ______________________________
3. ______________________________

I lay the following prayers at your feet as I rest in your goodness…

1. ______________________________
2. ______________________________
3. ______________________________

Date ___ / ___ / ___

But thanks be to God! He gives us
the victory through our Lord Jesus Christ.

-1 Corinthians 15:57

Father, I lift up the following in prayer as I start my day…

1. ______________________________
2. ______________________________
3. ______________________________

Father, I am thankful and grateful for….

1. ______________________________
2. ______________________________
3. ______________________________

Today I know you will you give me the strength to….

1. ______________________________

I praise you for all your mercies and blessings from today…

1. ______________________________
2. ______________________________
3. ______________________________

I lay the following prayers at your feet as I rest in your goodness…

1. ______________________________
2. ______________________________
3. ______________________________

Date ___ / ___ / ___

But Christ is faithful as the Son over God's house. And we are his house, if indeed we hold firmly to our confidence and the hope in which we glory.

-Hebrews 3:6

Father, I lift up the following in prayer as I start my day…

1. ______________________________
2. ______________________________
3. ______________________________

Father, I am thankful and grateful for….

1. ______________________________
2. ______________________________
3. ______________________________

Today I know you will you give me the strength to….

1. ______________________________

I praise you for all your mercies and blessings from today…

1. ______________________________
2. ______________________________
3. ______________________________

I lay the following prayers at your feet as I rest in your goodness…

1. ______________________________
2. ______________________________
3. ______________________________

Date ___ / ___ / ___

Jesus said to her, "I am the resurrection and the life.
The one who believes in me will live, even though they die;

-John 11:25

Father, I lift up the following in prayer as I start my day…

1. ______________________________
2. ______________________________
3. ______________________________

Father, I am thankful and grateful for….

1. ______________________________
2. ______________________________
3. ______________________________

Today I know you will you give me the strength to….

1. ______________________________

I praise you for all your mercies and blessings from today…

1. ______________________________
2. ______________________________
3. ______________________________

I lay the following prayers at your feet as I rest in your goodness…

1. ______________________________
2. ______________________________
3. ______________________________

Date ___ / ___ / ___

Do you not know that your body is a temple of the Holy Spirit, who is in you, whom you have received from God? You are not your own;

-1 Corinthians 6:19

Father, I lift up the following in prayer as I start my day…

1. ______________________________
2. ______________________________
3. ______________________________

Father, I am thankful and grateful for….

1. ______________________________
2. ______________________________
3. ______________________________

Today I know you will you give me the strength to….

1. ______________________________

I praise you for all your mercies and blessings from today…

1. ______________________________
2. ______________________________
3. ______________________________

I lay the following prayers at your feet as I rest in your goodness…

1. ______________________________
2. ______________________________
3. ______________________________

Date ___ / ___ / ___

Look, I am with you, and I will watch over you wherever you go, and I will bring you back to this land. For I will not leave you until I have done what I have promised you.

-Genesis 28:15

Father, I lift up the following in prayer as I start my day…

1. ____________________
2. ____________________
3. ____________________

Father, I am thankful and grateful for….

1. ____________________
2. ____________________
3. ____________________

Today I know you will you give me the strength to….

1. ____________________

I praise you for all your mercies and blessings from today…

1. ____________________
2. ____________________
3. ____________________

I lay the following prayers at your feet as I rest in your goodness…

1. ____________________
2. ____________________
3. ____________________

Date ___ / ___ / ___

For God did not send his Son into the world to condemn the world, but to save the world through him.

-John 3:17

Father, I lift up the following in prayer as I start my day…

1. ______________________________
2. ______________________________
3. ______________________________

Father, I am thankful and grateful for….

1. ______________________________
2. ______________________________
3. ______________________________

Today I know you will you give me the strength to….

1. ______________________________

I praise you for all your mercies and blessings from today…

1. ______________________________
2. ______________________________
3. ______________________________

I lay the following prayers at your feet as I rest in your goodness…

1. ______________________________
2. ______________________________
3. ______________________________

Congratulations!

You just completed 6 months of your *Four-Minute Prayer Journal.* Take a moment to reflect on all of the wonderful mercies, blessings, and answered prayers you have experienced over the last 6 months as you have strengthened your habit of connecting with the Lord in daily prayer.

Prayer is a powerful thing and we hope that the *Four-Minute Prayer Journal* has helped you strengthen your relationship with the Lord and that you are witnessing the incredible impact your prayers are having on not only your own life, but the lives of others. We know there were moments over the last 6 months where you were in a rush to start your day or had already laid down to rest, but you chose to spend time with the Father. What a testimonial to your faith and in the Lord and commitment to steadfast prayer! Thank you for all the prayers you have prayed. We know He hears them!

What impact has *The Four-Minute Prayer Journal* had on your life?

We would love to hear from you!
Email us at hello@FourMinutePrayerJournal.com

We also hope you have already ordered and received your next copy of your prayer journal so you can continue journaling and praying tomorrow.

Notes

Notes

Notes

Notes

Notes

Notes

Notes

Notes

Notes

Notes

Notes

Notes

Notes

REFERENCES

The following were used as references and inspiration for the development of the Four-Minute Prayer Journal:

Holy Bible

Holy Bible, New International Version®, NIV® Copyright ©1973, 1978, 1984, 2011 by Biblica, Inc.®

The Power of Positive Thinking

Peale, Norman Vincent. *The Power of Positive Thinking, (2003).* Touchstone, 2003. Print.

Counting Blessings Versus Burdens

Counting Blessings Versus Burdens: An Experimental Investigation of Gratitude and Subjective Well-being in Daily Life, Emmons and McCullough (2003)

Power of I Am

Olsteen, Joel. *The Power of I Am: Two Words That Will Change Your Life Today.* FaithWords, 2016. Print.

The Power of Habit

Duhigg, Charles. *The Power of Habit: Why We Do What We Do In Life and Business.* Duhigg, Charles. 2014. Print.